T0316571

Cambridge Elements ≡

Elements in the Economics of Emerging Markets
edited by
Bruno S. Sergi
Harvard University

CHINA'S FINANCE IN AFRICA

What and How Much?

Evelyn F. Wamboye
Pennsylvania State University

CAMBRIDGE
UNIVERSITY PRESS

CAMBRIDGE
UNIVERSITY PRESS

University Printing House, Cambridge CB2 8BS, United Kingdom

One Liberty Plaza, 20th Floor, New York, NY 10006, USA

477 Williamstown Road, Port Melbourne, VIC 3207, Australia

314–321, 3rd Floor, Plot 3, Splendor Forum, Jasola District Centre,
New Delhi – 110025, India

79 Anson Road, #06–04/06, Singapore 079906

Cambridge University Press is part of the University of Cambridge.

It furthers the University's mission by disseminating knowledge in the pursuit of
education, learning, and research at the highest international levels of excellence.

www.cambridge.org
Information on this title: www.cambridge.org/9781108789790
DOI: 10.1017/9781108893350

© Evelyn F. Wamboye 2020

First published 2020

A catalogue record for this publication is available from the British Library.

ISBN 978-1-108-78979-0 Paperback
ISSN 2631-8598 (online)
ISSN 2631-858X (print)

China's Finance in Africa

What and How Much?

Elements in the Economics of Emerging Markets

DOI: 10.1017/9781108893350
First published online: December 2020

Evelyn F. Wamboye
Pennsylvania State University
Author for correspondence: Evelyn F. Wamboye, efw10@psu.edu

Abstract: This Element provides a detailed analysis of official financing from China to Africa with special attention to the question of Africa's foreign finances policy. The findings reveal that Africa has an infrastructure gap and that Chinese finances are largely used to fund infrastructure projects. However, the majority of the funds come from loans mortgaged on Africa's natural resources. In addition, Chinese firms implement these projects, and many of the raw materials and much of the labor are imported from China. All of these facts call for Africa to institute a coherent foreign finances policy that ensures African countries fully benefit.

Keywords: Africa, Chinese finances, Tanzania, African infrastructure, African foreign finance policy

ISBNs: 9781108789790 (PB), 9781108893350 (OC)
ISSNs: 2631-8598 (online), 2631-858X (print)

Contents

1 Introduction: Africa in the Twenty-First Century – Changing Perceptions and Landscape

Africa, like many developing regions, has for many years entertained its fair share of development partners, both bilateral and multilateral. Each of these partners has presented unique strategic interests that have varied across the countries on the continent. Individuals of means and influence (including superstars in the entertainment industry and former government leaders), mainly from Western countries, in search of a place to showcase their philanthropic inclinations, have also found open arms in African countries. Thus, it is not surprising that to many foreigners and members of the international media, and within the research community, Africa is often dubbed a "hopeless continent," "hunger-, poverty- and disease-stricken" and "war-torn," and is often associated with aid dependency. Because of the unending civil strife and fragile interethnic relations across many African countries (such as Somalia, Rwanda, Liberia, Angola, Sudan and the Democratic Republic of Congo), and the donations of billions of dollars in foreign aid with no tangible results, one can feel justified to describe Africa in such terms.[1]

However, by 2009 the Africa narrative in the media and research communities had started changing. The narrative shifted from a concentration on the aid on which Africa depends to a focus on Africa rising, as portrayed in research publications such as *Africa Rising: How 900 Million African Consumers Offer More Than You Think* (Mahajan and Gunther, 2009) and *Africa Rising: A Tale of Growth, Inequality and Great Promise* (World Bank, 2014) and in headlines in prominent newspapers such as *The Economist (2011)* ("The Hopeful Continent – Africa Rising: After Decades of Slow Growth, Africa Has a Real Chance to Follow in the Footsteps of Asia") and the *Wall Street Journal*, which ran a series on Africa rising in 2011.[2] The African horizon has undoubtedly changed from bleak to bright. Aside from the skeptics of the Africa rising narrative ("'Africa Rising'? 'Africa Reeling' May Be More Fitting Now" [*New York Times*, 2016]), there is a good reason why the world now sees Africa as a hopeful rather than a hopeless continent. Africa has sustained a positive and meaningful growth trajectory (interrupted only by the COVID-19 world pandemic), it has made strides in innovation (see Figure 1), and it has forged new partners and markets, especially with China – a partnership that

---

[1] See the following studies on foreign aid in Africa: Bobba and Powell (2007), Boone (1996), Burnside and Dollar (2000), Collier and Dollar (2002), Easterly (2005), Easterly, Levine and Roodman (2004), Hansen and Tarp (2001), IMF and World Bank (2005), Karras (2006), Loxley and Sackey (2008), Marysee, Ansoms and Cassimon (2007), Minoiu and Reddy (2009), Moreira (2005), Svensson (1999), UNDP (2005).

[2] See articles by Connors (2011) and Gauthier-Villars (2011).

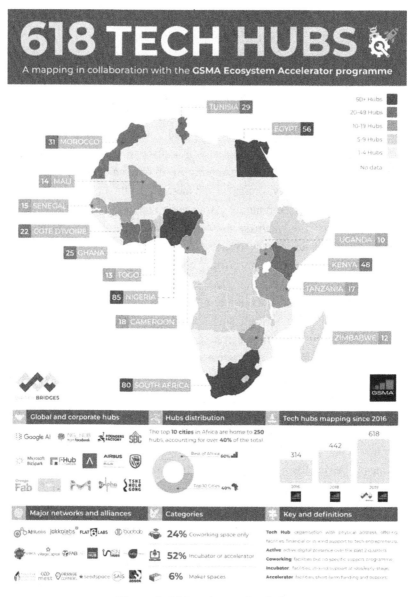

Figure 1 African innovation hubs

started in 2000 during the first Forum on China–Africa Cooperation (FOCAC) conference.

The landmark establishment of the FOCAC in 2000 ushered in a transformational economic and trade cooperation between China and Africa. The new era has been characterized by increased interaction with major changes in the volumes of trade and financial flows between China and Africa. The

FOCAC plans of action are regular biannual landmarks where policies and modalities of the partnership between China and Africa are articulated. The FOCAC also produces the Beijing Action Plans laying out the foundation and priority sectors for strengthening the relationship between China and African countries (Van Dijk, 2017). Between 2000 and 2014 China funded 2,390 projects across Africa totaling US$121.6 billion, constituting 34.3 percent of China's global development finance over that period. Most of the financing was concentrated in eastern (38.2 percent), central (25.1 percent) and western (20.4 percent) Africa. This regional distribution of financial flows roughly mirrored that of leading Western development finance sources over the same period.[3] For example, more than 40 percent of the aid provided to African countries by the United States of America (USA) went to East African countries in the same period.[4]

Before proceeding to the discussion of China's presence in Africa, the next section provides a contextual analysis of Africa's economic landscape in the context of Porter's (1990) Diamond Model. This is very important as it gives the reader a framework through which to evaluate the China-Africa relationship and areas that Africa's policy makers can capitalize for maximum benefit.

1.1 Africa's Competitive Advantage in the Context of the Diamond Model

In a speech at Peking University in China (November 2017) Makhtar Diop, the World Bank's vice president of the Africa Institute of South-South Cooperation and Development (ISSCAD), remarked that innovation is absolutely key to Africa's stability and growth and is necessary to achieve prosperity. Porter (1990) also emphasized innovation in his Diamond Model. In this model he posed a series of questions whose answers lay in the four broad attributes that collectively form a nation's diamond of competitive advantage: the nation's position in factors of production that include natural resources, human capital and physical capital (*factor conditions*); the nature of the home market's demand for domestic products or services (*demand conditions*); the presence or absence of internationally competitive intermediate input industries and other allied industries (*related and supporting industries*); and the presence of finance and government institutions that ensure the efficiency of the private sector (*firm strategy structure and rivalry*).[5] We evaluate each of these attributes in the context of African countries.

---

[3] See https://chinapower.csis.org/china-development-finance/.

[4] See https://explorer.usaid.gov/data.

[5] These questions include: Why are certain countries capable of consistent innovation through private enterprise and institutions of higher learning? Why do they continuously pursue improvements with a constant quest for more sophisticated sources of competitive advantage?

Table 1 Infrastructure development in Africa by sector, 2015–2019

Sectors	Share of projects by number (as percent				
	2015	**2016**	**2017**	**2018**	**2019**
Transport	37	34	36	39	33
Real estate	6	22	22	23	22
Energy and power	28	21	19	14	17
Shipping and ports		8	8	7	8
Water	8	4	5	5	6
Mining	7	3	3	7	6
Oil and gas	6	5	4	2	3
Other	8	3	3	3	5

Data source: Deloitte (2019)

1.1.1 A Nation's Position in Factors of Production

A number of studies show that Africa lags behind other developing regions in infrastructure development with an estimated infrastructure need of $130–170 billion a year and a financing gap of $68–108 billion (AfDB, 2015). Other studies reveal that Africa's infrastructure development remains suboptimal and costly with real consequences for structural transformation (Moller and Wacker, 2017; OECD, 2018; UNCTAD, 2011, 2015, 2017, 2018).

African countries are undoubtedly committed to ramping up investment in infrastructure despite the monumental task of making up for the lost decades (Deloitte, 2019). This is particularly so in transport, real estate, energy and power and shipping and ports (see Table 1). These efforts are exemplified at the subregional level (see Table 2) with East Africa leading the subregions (particularly in 2018–2019) in the number of projects; and Kenya, Tanzania, Egypt, Ethiopia and South Africa ranking as the top five countries on the continent (see Table 3).

Despite these efforts, poor investment in transportation and energy infrastructure persists. Reliable electricity access is a challenge (AfDB, 2019, 2020; Deloitte, 2019). For instance, in 2012 only eight of the fifty-two African countries had electricity access rates of between 85 percent (South Africa) and 100 percent (Algeria, Egypt, Libya, Mauritius, Morocco, Seychelles and Tunisia). Six countries (Botswana, Cameroon, Gabon, Ghana, Senegal and Sao Tome and Principe) had access rates between 51 percent and 75 percent. More than 50 percent of the population in the remaining 75 percent of the countries did not have access to electricity. In countries such as Chad, Liberia, Malawi, Sierra Leone, South Sudan, the Central African Republic and the Democratic

Table 2 Number and value of infrastructure projects in Africa, 2015–2019

		Number of projects				
Year	**Africa**	**Central Africa**	**East Africa**	**North Africa**	**West Africa**	**Southern Africa**
2015	301	23	61	29	79	109
2016	286	24	43	42	92	85
2017	303	20	71	40	79	93
2018	482	26	139	109	105	103
2019	452	16	182	87	75	92
		Value of projects (US$bn)				
2015	375	35.8	57.5	25.8	116.2	140
2016	324	7	27.4	76.1	119.8	93.4
2017	307	9.8	32.6	77.1	98.3	89.7
2018	471	26.9	87.1	148.3	82.8	125.4
2019	497	6.5	146.5	11.8	80.9	118.3

Data source: Deloitte (2019)

Table 3 Top five countries by number of projects, 2019

	Number of projects	**Value of projects (US$bn)**
Kenya	51	36
Tanzania	51	60.3
Egypt	49	103.1
Ethiopia	40	31.6
South Africa	37	65.7

Data source: Deloitte (2019)

Republic of Congo, 90 percent of the population does not have electricity access (AfDB, 2015).

In addition to the low investment in infrastructure, human capital development is low in Africa compared to other developing regions, and a significant mismatch has emerged between skills attained through schooling and those sought by employers across many African countries (AfDB, 2020). According to an AfDB report, only 33 percent of African countries have medium to high levels of human capital development; the remaining thirty-five countries have human capital development categorized as low (with an index below 0.55) (AfDB, 2015). Indeed, a number of African countries have made efforts to expand basic education (primary school) in response to the United Nation's

Millennium Development Goal 2 of achieving universal primary education, and have also increased the number of institutions of higher learning. In spite of this, African countries are yet to be strategic in creating specialized institutions that cater to individual countries' and the continent's needs, and that carve out global comparative advantage.

In fact, Porter (1990) argues that a nation does not inherit its most important factors of production such as skilled labor and a scientific base; rather it creates them through heavy and sustained investment, and such factors should be specialized in accordance to the needs of the industry for which the country has comparative advantage. In other words, African countries should strive to heavily invest in education that goes beyond basic primary and high school diplomas and general college to more specialized fields, which would create a pool of highly specialized world-class individuals that carve a niche for regions within the country and in the global marketplace. For example, countries like Kenya and Ethiopia with comparative advantage in long-distance marathons should establish institutions that specialize in sports medicine, while Tanzania with its lakes and minerals should invest in institutions whose core advantage is in mining engineering and related programs.

One area in which Africa has comparative advantage is its natural resources (fertile agricultural lands, oil, ores and minerals). But such resources have not served in Africa's best interest, particularly in getting it out of poverty and into the global value chain and up the global income ladder. This observation falls in line with Porter's Diamond model, which predicts that natural resources comprise a basic factor with no real competitive advantage in modern global competition. Also, empirical evidence from the most recent growth rates in Africa show that resource-poor countries are performing much better relative to those that are well endowed (see Table 4), reinforcing Porter's point that countries with an abundant supply of primary resources and cheap labor often deploy them inefficiently and settle on those advantages. Such veiled comparative advantage in natural resources hinders a country's ability to innovate and think outside the box, and has been the tragedy of many African nations. Moreover, there are a number of studies on the natural resources curse stemming from evidence in underdeveloped resource-rich countries, especially those in Africa (Auty, 1994; Frankel, 2010; Lederman and Maloney, 2003; Manzano and Rigobon, 2001).

1.1.2 The Nature of a Nation's Demand for Domestic Products or Services

The aforementioned factor conditions (appropriate skills, a scientific base and other factors enabling production) are important in enhancing a country's

Table 4 Real GDP growth in Africa

Region	2010–2014	2015	2016	2017	2018 (Estimated)	2019 (Projected)	2020 (Projected)
Central Africa	5	3.3	0.2	1.1	2.2	3.6	3.5
East Africa	5.9	6.5	5.1	5.9	5.7	5.9	6.1
North Africa	3.7	3.7	3.2	4.9	4.3	4.4	4.3
Southern Africa	3.8	1.6	0.7	1.6	1.2	2.2	2.8
West Africa	6.2	3.2	0.5	2.7	3.3	3.6	3.6
Africa	4.7	3.5	2.1	3.6	3.5	4	4.1
Sub-Saharan Africa	5.2	3.4	1.5	2.9	3.1	3.7	3.9
Oil-exporting countries	4.7	3.3	1.5	3.2	3.4	3.8	3.7
Oil-importing countries	4.6	3.7	3.1	4.2	3.8	4.3	4.5

Data source: Table 1.1 in AfDB (2019)

productive capacity. Nonetheless, a country must also meet the necessary demand conditions (Porter, 1990). The composition of the home market (in terms of size and purchasing power) and the sophistication of the buyers (who pressure companies to meet their superior tastes) shape the trajectory and pace of innovation and help to determine the composition of industries that give a country its competitive advantage.

African countries are heterogeneous, both across and within countries, which is a blessing and a curse. On one hand, it provides the opportunity for diverse tastes and a range of products and services that can be innovated; on the other hand, it negatively impacts the market size for any individual product and service, at least in the short term. With an estimated population of 1.2 billion and a population growth rate of 2.5 percent, Africa has a promising market size. Moreover, the urban population is expanding and the middle class is currently at 350 million people, estimated to reach 1.1 billion in 2060 (AfDB, 2014, 2019). Other demand condition indicators such as growth of private consumption and consumer spending are promising as well. For example, an African Development Bank report estimated an annual private consumption growth rate of 3.7 percent that started in 2010, and consumption spending accounting for 50–60 percent of Africa's economic growth (AfDB, 2014). In fact, consumer spending is expected to rise from $680 billion in 2008 to $2.2 trillion by 2030 (AfDB, 2014).

Additional evidence points to strong domestic demand, improved macroeconomic management, a growing middle class and increased political stability as the main drivers of the observed unprecedented economic growth rates in many African countries (AfDB, 2014, 2020; OECD, 2018). The questions now remain: how sophisticated are African consumers, and what policies have Africa countries put in place to ensure that private investors take advantage of this sophistication and market size?

1.1.3 Internationally Competitive Allied Industries

The third determinant of a nation's competitive advantage in Porter's (1990) Diamond model is internationally competitive related and supporting industries. Such industries deliver cost-effective inputs in an efficient, early and rapid manner (Porter, 1990). In order to increase efficiency and accelerate the pace of innovation, goods' producers must be located in a central cluster such as export-processing zones (EPZs), special economic zones (SEZs) and industrial parks. Such agglomeration enables close working relationships, quick and constant flow of information and the exchange of ideas (Porter, 1990). Of course allied industries go beyond intermediate input suppliers to include logistics, among other things. Many African countries now recognize the importance of such clusters and a number of them are now building industrial parks, rapid development zones and SEZs, and they are resuscitating or expanding EPZs (AfDB, 2017, 2020; OECD, 2018; Oyelaran-Oyeyinka and McCormick, 2007) and building transportation (road, rail, air and ports) networks that link these zones with markets. In fact, EPZs are not new in Africa. They have existed since the 1980s, but many of them lack the minimum institutional and physical infrastructure to be effective and attractive to foreign investors (AfDB, 2017; Farole and Akinci, 2011).

A major handicap for many African countries is the absence of internationally competitive domestic intermediate input suppliers. In fact, evidence suggests that foreign firms investing in African countries struggle to find local suppliers, forcing them to import from either their home countries or other international markets (AfDB, 2020; Drake-Brockman and Stephenson, 2012; Gebre-Egziabher, 2009; OECD, 2018; UNCTAD, 2019). Not only does this negatively impact the efficiency and cost of production, but it also stifles the backward and vertical linkages that could lead to technological spillovers to domestic producers in the short run and innovation in the long run (Jordaan, Douw and Qiang, 2020).

1.1.4 Presence of Quality Institutions

Institutions that ensure markets run smoothly and in turn create competitive advantage in a country, are another key factor in Porter's Diamond model. Stated as "firm strategy, structure and rivalry" in Porter (1990), this factor refers to "national circumstances and context that create strong tendencies in how companies are created, organized, and managed as well as what the nature of domestic rivalry will be." In the broader service sector context this can be considered as institutions such as financial, insurance and social (that support human capital development) institutions and governance that form the pillars of a well-functioning market system.

The institutions factor is the area in which African countries have the biggest weakness. Indeed, political stability in Africa as measured by improvements in indicators of governance (safety and security, the rule of law, political participation, human rights, public sector management, the business environment and social inclusion) has experienced some positive changes since 2001 (AfDB, 2014, 2020; OECD, 2018). The most notable changes have occurred in political participation, with sixteen countries either revising or implementing new constitutions, and many others having peaceful and credible elections with smooth

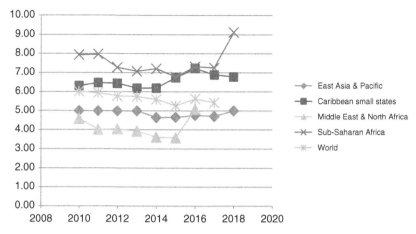

Figure 2 Interest rate spread (lending rate minus deposit rate, in percent)
Data source: Author's calculations based on data from the World Bank's World
Development Indicators database

transitions (AfDB and OECD, 2006; Wamboye and Sergi, 2019).[6] Nonetheless,
some improvements remain to be made, particularly in reforming the judicial
system (maintaining the rule of law and contract enforcement), eliminating
corruption, reducing the time it takes to issue a business license or permit,
and enhancing political stability (AfDB, 2019). Other areas that could be
improved include government regulations on businesses, simplified tax laws
(WEF, 2017) and management of taxation and tax revenues (UNDP, 2017).

Improving access to credit and insurance has a big impact on business
development and hedging against risks (AfDB, 2018; Beck and Cull, 2014;
Beck, Fuchs and Uy, 2009). Many African countries have made strides in
financial market inclusion (especially in the banking sector), thanks to the
introduction of mobile money banking through platforms like Kenya's
MPESA (OECD, 2018). Despite this, general financial sector development
and the savings rate in African countries are still low relative to other regions
and countries, and the lending rates are exorbitantly high (Beck et al., 2009; see
Figure 2). Moreover, due to imperfect information in the banking sector, the
collateral required to extend credit excludes many potential investment projects.
Further still, the financial markets for short-term liquidity such as stock markets
are underdeveloped or missing altogether in some countries (Issahaku, 2019;

---

[6] These countries have either revised or implemented new constitutions since 2000, with years of
revision or implementation in parentheses: Angola (2010), Comoros (2018), the Democratic
Republic of Congo (2006), Djibouti (2010), Egypt (2014), Ivory Coast (2016), Kenya (2010),
Libya (2011), Madagascar (2010), Niger (2010), Rwanda (2003), Senegal (2016), Somalia
(2012), Sudan (2005), Tunisia (2014) and Zimbabwe (2013).

Wamboye and Mookerjee, 2014). The insurance sector, which enables borrowers and investors to hedge against risks, is equally underdeveloped with a very low penetration rate (Ngwu, Ogbechie and Otanya, 2019; WEF, 2017). All these factors constrain access to capital that is essential in spurring innovation and increasing entrepreneurial activities in Africa (Christopoulos and Tsionas, 2004; Levine, 2004).

1.2 Drivers of Economic Growth and Development in Africa

Despite some of the handicaps mentioned earlier and before the interruption from the COVID-19 world pandemic, economic growth in many African countries has averaged more than 5 percent for more than a decade (see Figure 3; AfDB, 2018, 2019, 2020; OECD, 2018). This is in comparison to the dismissal growth rates of the 1980s and early 1990s. But the growth has not translated into economic development that would lift many of these countries out of poverty and into the ranks of middle-income countries similar to what was observed in the Asian tigers and now China (OECD, 2018). Moreover, a larger percentage of African economies is in the informal sector; this sector accounts for 50–80 percent of the economy, 60–80 percent of employment and up to 90 percent of new jobs created (AfDB, 2018). This leaves the formal sector as low as 20 percent of the economy in some countries.

Notwithstanding the informality of these economies, history has shown that meaningful economic growth accompanied by economic development must be driven by the industrial sector and, more specifically, the manufacturing subsector. Contrary to expectations, the average growth rates between 2000 and 2018 of the manufacturing subsector in sub-Saharan Africa (SSA) (6.8 percent) and the industry sector (6.2 percent) were much lower than the services sector (10.3 percent), and in fact, the growth trend (see Figures 4A and 4B) in the manufacturing subsector was more volatile than that in the services sector. Furthermore, the value added in GDP of Africa's services sector averaged around 47 percent in SSA and 50 percent in the Middle East and North Africa (MENA) between 2000 and 2018, suggesting that the observed growth in many African countries is driven largely by the services sector rather than the manufacturing subsector (see Table 5). In line with the data on sectoral growth rates, the manufacturing subsector's value added in GDP averaged 11 (15) percent in SSA (MENA), and that of agriculture was roughly 17 percent and 5 percent during the 2000–2018 period in SSA and MENA, respectively.

Given the heterogeneity of African countries in terms of resource endowment, legal origin, level of economic development, level of economic diversification, quality of institutions, differences in government policy space and other

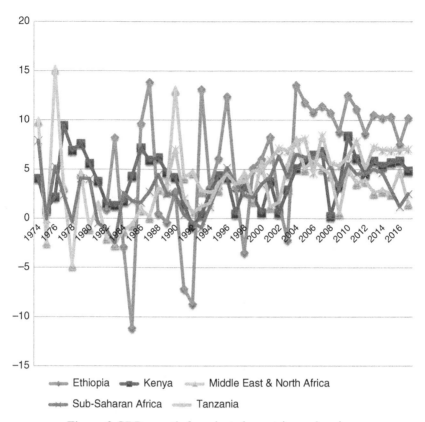

Figure 3 GDP growth for selected countries and regions
Data source: Author's calculations based on the World Bank's World Development
Indicators online data set

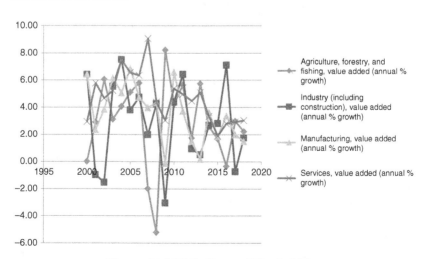

Figure 4A Middle East and North Africa
Data source: Author's calculations based on data from the World Bank's World
Development Indicators database

Table 5 Average sectoral share in GDP in Africa (2000–2018)

	Sub-Saharan Africa	Middle East and North Africa
Agriculture, forestry and fishing, value added (percent of GDP)	16.67	5.22
Industry (including construction), value added (percent of GDP)	27.48	45.45
Manufacturing, value added (percent of GDP)	10.75	14.88
Services, value added (percent of GDP)	49.69	47.45

Data source: Author's calculations based on data from the World Bank's World Development Indicators database

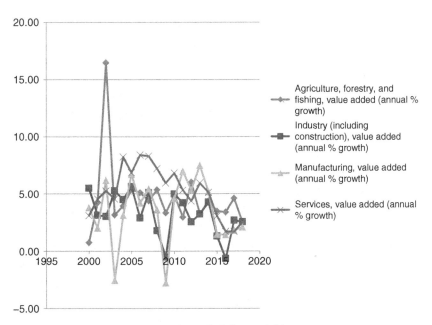

Figure 4B Sub-Saharan Africa

Data source: Author's calculations based on data from the World Bank's World Development Indicators database

salient features such as ethnic diversity, it comes as no surprise that sectoral composition in GDP and GDP growth rates vary across countries and subregions and between oil-exporting and non-oil-exporting countries (see Table 4). For example, GDP growth in North Africa was lower than that of SSA for the

2010–2014 period at 3.7 percent and 5.2 percent, respectively. The difference could largely be attributed to the Arab Spring that raged across the MENA region and negatively impacted economic fundamentals between 2010 and 2012. However, North African countries rebounded in 2015, and their GDP growth has been outpacing that of SSA ever since. Among SSA's subregions, East Africa stands out as the fastest growing, with the GDP growth rate averaging above 5 percent since 2010. Southern African countries had the lowest growth rate, which has barely reached 2 percent since 2010. The observed difference in GDP growth rate is also palpable across countries in the region. For instance, within the East Africa subregion, it is evident that Ethiopia has the highest GDP growth rate (above 10 percent since 2004) followed by Tanzania (around 7 percent) and Kenya (about 5 percent) (see Figure 3).

Sectoral shares vary across the subregions as well. As indicated in Table 5, the services sector is the biggest in Africa in terms of its values added in GDP. For example, between 2000 and 2018 (latest data) the sector's share in GDP averaged around 50 percent in SSA and 47 percent in MENA. This was followed by the industry sector, which is much higher in the MENA region (45 percent) relative to SSA (27 percent). The agriculture sector has the lowest share in the MENA region's GDP (lower than the manufacturing subsector), while the manufacturing subsector has the lowest value added in SSA's GDP, which averaged about 17 percent and 5 percent during the 2000–2018 period in SSA and MENA, respectively.

The variations in sector composition in GDP are also observed at the country level. Again, using examples from three East African countries, it is evident that the agriculture share in GDP is higher in Ethiopia (40 percent), while the services is the biggest sector in both Kenya (47 percent) and Tanzania (44 percent). Not surprising, the share of the manufacturing sub-sector in GDP is lower in all three countries; with Ethiopia at 5 percent and Kenya and Tanzania at 10 percent and 9 percent, respectively. However, when we evaluate the sectoral composition of these countries in terms of growth rates (Table 6) the picture is somehow different. For instance, industry is the fastest-growing sector in both Ethiopia (13 percent) and Tanzania (9 percent), largely driven by the manufacturing subsector (11 percent for Ethiopia and 8 percent for Tanzania). On the contrary, the growth rate of the services sector is higher in Kenya (5 percent) compared to the agriculture and industry sectors, albeit at a lower level than Ethiopia (11 percent) and Tanzania (8 percent). In general, Kenya exhibits the lowest growth rate across all three sectors, including the manufacturing subsector, compared to Ethiopia and Tanzania.

Table 6 Average sectoral growth rate and shares in GDP (2000–2018)

	Ethiopia	Kenya	Tanzania
Agriculture, forestry and fishing, value added (percent of GDP)	40.06	26.61	25.71
Industry (including construction), value added (percent of GDP)	13.61	17.40	23.40
Manufacturing, value added (percent of GDP)	4.80	10.46	8.92
Services, value added (percent of GDP)	39.18	47.31	43.67
Agriculture, forestry and fishing, value added (annual percent growth)	6.18	3.21	4.44
Industry (including construction), value added (annual percent growth)	13.09	4.74	8.88
Manufacturing, value added (annual percent growth)	10.90	3.13	7.65
Services, value added (annual percent growth)	10.89	5.55	6.77

Data source: Author's calculations based on the World Bank's World Development Indicators online database

Aside from the sectoral shares, evidence shows that the biggest driver of Africa's GDP and hence its growth is the robust domestic consumer demand in many countries, especially in non-oil-exporting countries (Signe, 2018), followed by a surge in commodity prices (Leke, Lund, Roxburgh and Van Wamelen, 2010). Other aspects that have contributed to this growth include reduction in the inflation rate, debt relief initiatives in the formerly heavily indebted poor countries, political stability, fiscal prudence, liberation of the trade and financial sectors and proliferation of information and communication technologies (ICTs) (AfDB, 2020; OECD, 2018; Wamboye and Sergi, 2019).

Now that the COVID-19 pandemic has brought the entire globe to a standstill, halting all wheels of the economic engine and increasing unemployment rates to levels that rival only those of the Great Depression, it has now become a waiting game to see the extent to which African countries will be impacted. Undoubtedly consumer demand has been hit hard globally as people lose wealth and sources of income and commodity prices – especially that of oil – tumble. This suggests that Africa, which does not have a consumer safety net (similar to that in developed and emerging economies), and whose export basket consists largely of primary commodities and has a high dependency on the tourism subsector, will be negatively impacted with real consequences for the poverty rate and the economic growth trajectory of most countries on the continent.[7]

2 Literature Review: China's Engagement in Africa

Until the early 2000s African countries received foreign aid with very little in the form of economic development to show for it. Traditional donors – mainly member nations of the Organization of the Petroleum Exporting Countries (OECD), the International Monetary Fund (IMF) and the World Bank – have provided aid to these countries with wholesale conditionalities meant to increase the aid's effectiveness, but it is now questionable whether such efforts yield any tangible results, especially in terms of moving these countries up the global economic ladder. The critical questions that should now be asked are: Why has Africa been in a perpetual state of dependency? Is it the funding policies of traditional development partners that have perpetuated Africa's hopeless state, or is it Africa's lack of a strategic pro-development foreign finances policy?

Until recently Africa provided a rich ground, especially for development economists, to investigate various dimensions of the relationship between foreign aid and economic development and growth. Among the most popular topics were the role and impact of foreign aid in the context of traditional donors.[8] Researchers often attempted to provide explanations for why foreign aid has not been effective in African countries and hence the continent's continued dependency on aid. Some scholars went to the extreme of concluding that climatic conditions in Africa were the major impediment to the effectiveness of aid on the continent (Dalgaard, Hansen and Tarp, 2004; Easterly, Levine and Roodman, 2004). Others insisted the cure to Africa's aid dependency was to provide more aid (Sachs, 2005). But the recent turn in Africa's growth trajectory (from hopelessness to promising) and the growing size of the middle class has brought under question all the assessments and prescriptions in the Africa foreign aid literature.

---

[7] According to AfDB (2020), poverty on the continent had been projected (prior to COVID-19) to decline from 0.71 percentage points in 2020 to 0.67 percentage points in 2021. But when the effects of COVID-19 are accounted for extreme poverty is projected to increase by 2.14 percentage points in the baseline scenario in 2020 and by 2.84 percentage points in the worst-case scenario with a possibility of climbing as high as 3.63 percentage points in 2021. The report concludes that in the worst-case scenario an additional 49.2 million Africans could be pushed into extreme poverty.

[8] See Bobba and Powell (2007); Boone (1996); Burnside and Dollar (2000); Collier and Dollar (2002); Easterly (2005); Easterly et al. (2004); Hansen and Tarp (2001); IMF and World Bank (2005); Karras (2006); Loxley and Sackey (2008); Marysee et al. (2007); Minoiu and Reddy (2009); Moreira (2005); Svensson (1999).

What has changed? Have the climatic conditions become more conducive, or have the development partners provided the required level of aid necessary for takeoff into sustained growth and development? On the contrary, most African countries still have tropical climates and many countries on the continent remain highly dependent on foreign aid relative to other developing regions and countries. However, one thing is for sure; African countries have found new development partners and have diversified their sources of foreign funding. The most prominent of these partners is China. Consequently, the literature review in this Element focuses exclusively on the role of China's engagement in Africa and its contribution to the economic changes taking place in many of the countries on the continent.

China's role in Africa as a development partner dates back to the early 1950s and 1960s when it provided economic assistance to the newly independent African nations as a sign of its resistance to imperialism and colonialism (Samy, 2010). For example, in 1967, China agreed to provide an interest-free loan of $406 million (RMB 988 million) to Tanzania and Zambia for the construction of the Tanzania-Zambia railroad (TaZaRa) (Ministry of Foreign Affairs of the People's Republic of China, 2018). The funding of TaZaRa marked the beginning of diplomatic and economic ties between China and Africa. Other financial support from China to Africa followed, albeit very sporadic and obscure. The present-day China-Africa relationship that has caught the attention of Western analysts and researchers alike started with the first ministerial conference of the FOCAC held in October 2000 in Beijing.

The China-Africa cooperation narrative has been developing for almost twenty years now, moving at a very fast pace (compared to more than fifty years with OECD development partners), with researchers playing catch-up. As a result, literature in this area is very limited. This literature can be categorized in four crude themes: China's motive/aid policy in Africa (Alden, 2006; Glosny, 2006; Kachiga, 2013; Naim, 2007; Samy, 2010; Shinn and Eisenman, 2012; Signe, 2018; Sun, 2014; Taylor, 2006; Tull, 2006; Van Dijk, 2017), the role and nature of China's finance in Africa (Brautigam and Gallagher, 2014; Foster, Butterfield, Chuan and Pushak, 2008), the potential contribution of China's financial support to the debt crisis in Africa (Niambi, 2019), and Africa's foreign aid policy in the context of China's finance (Osakwe, 2017; Samy, 2010).We explore these themes in the next paragraphs.

2.1 China's Motive or Finance Policy in Africa

Scholars offer competing perceptions of China's motive or rather China's finance policy in Africa. To some, these perceptions are rooted in deep-seated ideologies that stem from the Cold War era of communism versus capitalism and the mistrust that came with it. Western policy makers who view China as a communist state by default mistrust China's intentions. However, aside from the ideology, the mistrust could be based on fear or panic as China has displaced OECD member countries' diplomatic and capitalistic soft power in many SSA countries (Rotberg, 2008). As COVID-19 has unmasked, the world (including Western nations) heavily depends on China for manufactured products (including things such as masks) and fresh capital. Despite the realities of China's importance to the rest of the world (including developed countries), Western analysts and policy makers see China as a rogue nation hungry for Africa's rich natural resources without development intentions, which ironically are the same accusations that could be leveled against Western countries after more than fifty years of extracting natural resources from Africa and worsening the development status of nearly all the countries on the continent. Hence it is not surprising that from African leaders' perspective, China is a development partner whose relationship is based on the principles of neutrality, friendship, mutual benefit and equality, and China offers an alternative development model to the Washington Consensus.

China's finance policy in Africa has evolved, at least in its implementation, since the 1960s when Premier Zhou Enlai outlined the guiding principles of the China-Africa relationship. However, in some ways it is no different from Africa's relationship to OECD member countries as regards to accessing Africa's natural resources. For example, similar to China, British and French interests provide significant amounts of low-interest loans through their commercial banks to African countries richly endowed with oil and ores to gain preferential access. What sets China apart from traditional donors is its principles of mutual cooperation, developing partnerships, noninterference in the host government's domestic affairs and not linking its commercial relationships to any standards of conduct or requirement to adhere to certain economic and governance measures.

To understand China's finance policy in Africa we have to go back to Premier Enlai's speech in Ghana and Mali in 1964 when he outlined the eight principles that inform China's finance policy in Africa today:

I. The Chinese government always bases itself on the principle of equality and mutual benefit in providing aid to other countries. It never regards such aid as a kind of unilateral alms but as something mutual.

II. In providing aid to other countries, the Chinese government strictly respects the sovereignty of the recipient countries, and never attaches any conditions or asks for any privileges.

III. China provides economic aid in the form of interest-free or low-interest loans and extends the time limit for repayment when necessary so as to lighten the burden of the recipient country as far as possible.

IV. In providing aid to other countries, the purpose of the Chinese government is not to make the recipient country dependent on China but to help them embark step by step on the road of self-reliance and independent economic development.

V. The Chinese government tries its best to help the recipient countries build projects, which require less investment while yielding quicker results, so that the recipient governments may increase their income and accumulate capital.

VI. The Chinese government provides the best equipment and material of its own manufacture at international market prices. If the equipment or material are not up to the agreed specifications and quality, the Chinese government undertakes to replace them.

VII. In providing any technical assistance, the Chinese government will see to it that the personnel of the recipient countries fully master such technique.

VIII. The experts dispatched by China to help in construction in the recipient countries will have the same standard of living as the experts of the recipient countries. The Chinese experts are not allowed to make any special demands or enjoy any special amenities. (Ministry of Foreign Affairs of the People's Republic of China)

While these principles provide the basis for China's Africa foreign aid policy, the implementation has evolved to meet Beijing's changing commercial and political needs. The biggest factor in African countries' preference for China over traditional donors is China's principles of noninterference in domestic affairs and nonattachment of any conditions on its finances. In practice, China has effectively employed this principle to forge partnerships in countries previously shunned by OECD member countries and the IMF/World Bank because of not adhering to prescribed conditions. However, China also has provided exceptions to this principle in subtle ways to protect its interests in some countries.

Angola and Sudan provide ideal case studies for the China finance policy in Africa. Both countries engaged in long civil wars and were in dire need of foreign funding to rebuild and jump-start their economies. In 2004 China was willing to provide a loan to dos Santos's corrupt government in Angola to rebuild the country after the civil war when the IMF and the World Bank were only willing to provide the loan on conditions that the government addressed transparency and accountability concerns, and also delayed rebuilding its infrastructure until both its fiscal and monetary policy issues were addressed (Jiang, 2008). On the other hand, OECD member countries had deserted Sudan because of instability and the humanitarian and safety concerns stemming from the civil war. Only China was willing to step in and provide the much-needed funding to rescue the Sudanese economy, and China invested in Sudan's oil fields in the 1990s (Jiang, 2008). However, when China felt its interests were threatened by the ongoing civil war, it employed subtle behind-the-scenes intervention through dialogue and consultation to influence Khartoum to agree to a peace agreement that resulted in Sudan granting South Sudan autonomy in 2005.

Contrary to how China portrays its engagements and policy in Africa, Western governments and policy makers characterize China as a malign force and its finance policy in Africa as neocolonial, rogue, nontransparent, nondemocratic and toxic – only interested in using aid as leverage to access Africa's natural resources without real intentions for development (Jiang, 2008; Naim, 2007; Rotberg, 2008; Samy, 2010). There is also an intense fear among Western governments and policy makers that China's aid conditionalities could destroy the funding and the years of promoting strong institutions and good governance that OECD member countries have invested in Africa (Hubbard, 2008). Western bilateral and multilateral donors view China's principle of noninterference in particular as undermining their efforts to reduce corruption and improve governance in Africa (Jiang, 2008; Rotberg, 2008; Samy, 2010). This principle enables China to finance repressive regimes (such as Angola and Sudan) without any conditions. As a result corruption, environmental degradation and human right abuses thrive at the expense of the masses while enriching and propping up despots.

Other scholars caution against passing quick judgments on China's finance policy in Africa, arguing that it is difficult to draw out China's real intentions (Glosny, 2006). This begs the question of how effective Western policies and conditions have been in helping ordinary Africans and African countries develop given their refusal to fund infrastructure projects that are well known to drive economic growth and development. As cited previously, literature on foreign aid has shown that these policies and conditions have been highly ineffective.

Indeed, contrary to Premier Enlai's seventh principle, there is evidence that China does not allow technology transfer and capacity building in African countries since much of its aid is tied to importing material from China and using Chinese firms to implement China-funded projects as part of the mutual benefit principle. Moreover, Chinese firms tend to use workers imported from

China (Jiang, 2008) and in instances when locals are employed, they are exploited with poor working conditions and relatively low wages, which stands in stark contrast to conditions in OECD member countries' firms whose workforces comprise more than 70 percent Africans and are highly engaged in local communities (Jiang, 2008). An excerpt from Lee and Shalmon (2008: 122) highlights these issues:

> China is reluctant to hire local workers, both for management and for unskilled jobs. Therefore, most of the people who work in Chinese enterprises in Angola, as well as in other parts of Africa, are Chinese nationals. They live in their own enclaves, do not learn the local language, go to Chinese schools, and stand apart from the native population.

In addition, evidence shows that a larger percentage of Chinese imports from Africa are crude oil and ores and the loans to many African countries are escrowed on Africa's natural resources (oil and ores) and agricultural output (Jian, 2008; Lee and Shalmon, 2008), lending weight to the critique that China is using its foreign aid and other loans as a gateway to access Africa's natural resources.

Western media and analysts have, perhaps not surprisingly, been generally very critical of China's rising influence in Africa. Of course, Western countries have been the dominant players on the continent for a very long time and China's emergence both poses a threat to their dominance and stokes fear of the unknown. The African reaction has been mixed. Africa's activists and researchers have been more cautious, worried about the possible negative repercussions on governance, the environment, human rights and overall economic development. Some have even raised concerns of a new form of neocolonialism. But China has won African leaders' hearts and minds because of two major aspects of its financing and partnership: its policy of noninterference in domestic affairs and economic packages that come without prescribed economic and governance conditions. African leaders see what is popularly termed on the continent as the "Beijing Consensus" (Ramo, 2004) as an attractive alternative economic development model to the Washington Consensus and decades of a disappointing neoliberal model and its accompanying structural adjustment programs (Samy, 2010). In the eyes of African leaders, China is a developing country as their nations are, and has shared development experiences without the intimidating legacy of European imperialism. Moreover, China provides opportunity for a competitive funding environment and its funding is less volatile and more predictable relative to that of OECD member countries (Hamann and Bulir, 2001; Samy, 2010). This in turn has made African leaders blindly embrace China's finance policy, allowing Beijing, similar to OECD donors, to dictate the rules and direction of the game.

African leaders' positive attitude toward China reflects the perceptions of the majority of the African public. By all indications, China has earned goodwill in Africa (from north to south and east to west), particularly because of its funding of infrastructure projects, foreign direct investment, and the cheaper cost of its exports to Africa. In 2016 Afrobarometer conducted a survey across thirty-six African countries drawn from the five regions (central, east, north, west and south) of the continent (Lekorwe, Chingwete, Okuru and Samson, 2016). The survey asked several questions to a sample drawn from the African public and took into consideration age, gender, economic status, education and living location (rural or urban). In addition to asking what factors made people perceive China positively or negatively, the survey included questions on economic contribution, political influence, China's development model and China's external influence, among others.

The survey results showed that roughly 63 percent of the African public views China positively because of its economic contribution and political influence on the continent. The ratings were as high as 84 percent in Niger and 92 percent in Mali. In fact, about 58 percent of African countries rated China's model of economic development as second best after the USA model, while 25 percent rated China's model as their preferred model of economic development. In terms of China's external influence, 47 percent of the respondents found it helpful, though that of the USA was ranked higher at 54 percent and that of the former colonial powers ranked third at 45 percent. The majority of the respondents (about 69 percent) felt that China exerted economic influence in Africa. These ratings were consistent across gender, age, residency location, education and economic status.

Overall, evidence shows that China's finance policy in Africa has been well received by African leaders and the majority of the African public. The biggest factor contributing to the positive image is China's funding of infrastructure projects, an area Western donors abandoned long ago in favor of budget funding (OECD, 2019). Data from the Afrobarometer survey shows that infrastructure funding was favored by 32 percent of the African public, followed by affordable Chinese products (23 percent) and business investment (16 percent). The factors that contributed to a negative view of China's presence in Africa were the quality of its products (35 percent), taking jobs/ business away from Africans (14 percent) and the extraction of natural resources (10 percent).

Regardless of how you interpret China's finance policy in Africa, its strategy is no different from that of other donors and development partners who have used aid to exploit Africa's natural resources (Mourdoukoutas, 2018; Shinn and Eisenman, 2012; Tull, 2006). Most of these traditional donors fear that China's finance policy in Africa is not in alignment with those of other bilateral and multilateral donors from the developed world (Hubbard, 2008). However, by all indications China hardly wants to colonize Africa, but it has immense mercantilist ambitions. It is in need of raw material to feed its massive industrial surge (Rotberg, 2008). Moreover, unlike the United Kingdom, France and other OECD member countries that tend to be concentrated in a handful of countries (especially former colonies in the case of the United Kingdom and France), China, like the United States, is an equal opportunity lender whose reach extends to every African country that supports its one-China principle.

China has used its finances effectively as a form of soft power, a tool of diplomacy and an instrument to meet its political and economic goals (Brautigam, 2008; Kurlantzick, 2007; Samy, 2010; Sun, 2014). Through aid it has gained support for political recognition on the world stage and won a bid for its claim to the United Nations Security Council seat once held by Taiwan (1949–1971). China has used its finances to boost its trade and win profitable infrastructure projects for its state-owned companies (Brautigam, 2008), and to access Africa's rich natural resources (including oil and ores) for its massive industrial sector.

2.2 The Role and Nature of China's Finance in Africa

On November 4, 2006, six years after the first ministerial conference of FOCAC, President Hu Jintao welcomed government leaders and representatives from forty-eight African countries at the Great Hall of the People in Beijing with a speech that spelled hope for the development of African countries. It hit all of the important notes these leaders wanted to hear about: increasing trade volume, foreign direct investment and preferential loans, canceling debt, and providing financial assistance and technical expertise for social development.[9] The speech, though heavy on trade and investment, provided a glimpse into the extent of Chinese engagements in African countries. One of the key elements that was not reflected in the speech, a distinguishing factor of Chinese finance versus that of OECD member countries, was funding for infrastructure (transport, information and communications technology, energy and water).

China is an equal opportunity lender. Its funding patterns in terms of sectors and composition of countries are similar to those of the USA. While China is in nearly every African country that upholds the one-China policy and its funding is dispersed in nearly every sector, the list of its top ten countries is no different from that of OECD member countries; they tend to be resource rich, with a few

---

[9] See the China Ministry of Foreign Affairs website: www.fmprc.gov.cn/zflt/eng/tptb/t404225.htm.

Table 7A Top ten recipients of Chinese finance in Africa, 2000–2014

Country	Amount (US$bn)
Angola	21.20
Ethiopia	12.30
Sudan	5.60
Kenya	5.20
Democratic Republic of Congo	4.90
Republic of Congo	4.70
Nigeria	4.70
Ghana	4.60
Cameroon	4.50
Equatorial Guinea	4.40

Source: Figure 3 in Brautigam and Hwang (2016)

exceptions such as Kenya and Ethiopia (Brautigam and Hwang, 2016; see Tables 7A and 7B). Also the sectors that get the most funding are infrastructure (transportation, and information and communications technology) and natural resources (energy and mining) [see Figures 4A and 4B].

As shown in Figure 5, the transportation infrastructure (28 percent) and energy generation (20 percent) sectors account for 58 percent of China's total development finance in Africa.[10]

A large percentage of the funding in the transportation subsector is for roads (40 percent) and rail (39 percent), while that in energy is for hydropower plants (46 percent) and electrical grids (28 percent) (see Table 8). This composition of development support appeals to Beijing's twin goals of connecting African markets with the Chinese economy and enhancing China's access to natural resources. It is also consistent with what distinguishes China from traditional donors – China focuses on big physical projects while traditional donors are more mundane, devoting much of their funding (more than 40 percent) to the social sector (basic education, basic health care, population and reproductive health, water supply and sanitation, government and civil society) (OECD, 2019).

2.2.1 Foreign Aid and Loans

China offers aid in three forms: grants (which include in-kind transfers of services, goods and, in some cases, cash), zero-interest loans, and low-interest concessional loans with subsidized interest rates (Brautigam,

---

[10] Refer to https://chinapower.csis.org/china-development-finance/.

Table 7B Top ten recipients of OECD member countries ODA (USD million, receipts from all donors, net ODA receipts), 2014–2016

Country	2014	2015	2016	Three-year average	Percent of all recipients
Ethiopia	3,584	3,234	4,074	3,630	7 percent
Egypt	3,538	2,499	2,130	2,722	5 percent
Tanzania	2,651	2,582	2,318	2,517	5 percent
Nigeria	2,479	2,432	2,501	2,470	5 percent
Kenya	2,661	2,464	2,189	2,438	5 percent
Democratic Republic of Congo	2,400	2,599	2,107	2,369	5 percent
Morocco	2,240	1,481	1,992	1,905	4 percent
Mozambique	2,106	1,815	1,531	1,817	4 percent
South Sudan	1,964	1,675	1,590	1,743	3 percent
Uganda	1,634	1,628	1,757	1,673	3 percent
Other recipients	28,827	28,635	27,764	28,409	55 percent
Total ODA recipients	54,083	51,044	49,954	51,694	100 percent

Source: Table 2.1.1 in OECD (2019), "Development Aid at a Glance: Africa"

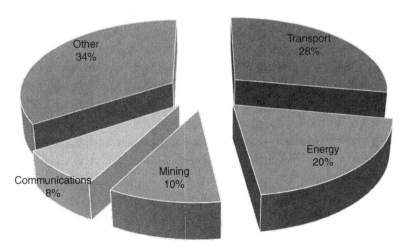

Figure 5 Top four sectors receiving Chinese finances in Africa, 2000–2014
Source: Figure 4 in Brautigam and Hwang (2016)

Table 8 Projects benefiting from Chinese finance by sector (2000–2014)

Energy sector		Transportation sector	
Project	**Share (percent)**	**Project**	**Share (percent)**
Hydropower	46	Road	40
Power lines	28	Rail	39
Gas pipelines	12	Air	11
Gas power plants	6	Water	8
Other	8	Other	2

Source: Figure 5 in Brautigam and Hwang (2016)

2008; Rotberg, 2008). The foreign aid (similar to the official development assistance (ODA) that OECD member countries disburse to developing countries) is disbursed under the category of *Other Official Assistance*. China also provides loans at market rates, some of which are mortgaged on future revenues from commodities (oil and ores), agricultural goods (Ethiopia), energy (Ghana) and rail transportation (Kenya) (Brautigam and Hwang, 2016; Lee and Shalmon, 2008; Signe, 2018).[11] China uses two models of financing: strategic partnerships and resource-backed package financing. Five major instruments are used in development assistance: lines of credit to Chinese multinational corporations (MNCs), export credit, resource-backed loans, the China Africa Development Fund and Chinese overseas SEZs. Two Chinese state-owned policy banks founded in 1994 provide financing (including loans) to Africa, with each specializing in a niche area.

The Export Import Bank of China (Exim Bank) provides the bulk of funding for export facilitation (Brautigam, 2008). As indicated on the bank's website, the business scope of Exim Bank includes providing short-, medium- and long-term loans for foreign trade and China's "going global" endeavors, which include export credit, import credit, loans for offshore contracts and overseas investment, Chinese government concessional loans, and preferential export buyer's credit.

The second policy bank is the China Development Bank (CDB), which was incorporated in December 2008 and designated as a development finance institution by the State Council in March 2015. The bank's biggest shareholder is the Ministry of Finance (MoF) of the People's Republic of China (holding

---

[11] Some authors claim that Chinese finance is not out of line and that it has interest rates found in the global capital markets (Degele and Seshagiri, 2019).

36.54 percent of the shares). This suggests that the MoF has the largest influence on the bank's operations. The bank website describes the CDB as the world's largest development finance institution and states that the CDB provides medium- to long-term financing facilities that serve China's major long-term economic and social development strategies. It also lists the China-Africa Development Fund (CADF) and the CDB Development Fund as its subsidiaries.

The CADF was established in 2006 as one of the eight policy measures proposed by the Chinese government during the Beijing Summit of FOCAC with the sole objective of encouraging and supporting Chinese companies to invest in Africa. It started its operations in 2007 with an initial operating capital of $5 billion that was increased to $10 billion in 2015. As indicated on the CADF website, the fund provides active support for economic and trade cooperation between China and African countries, focusing on a group of industrial parks and agricultural, infrastructure, manufacturing and resource-development projects.

Investment projects funded under the CADF are selected according to the "strategic necessity of investment, financial balance of projects and sustainability of corporate development" as the fundamental principles with priority given to the construction of the "three major networks" (high-speed rail, motorways and regional aviation) in Africa, industrialization, production capacity cooperation between China and African countries, the entry of Chinese equipment manufacturers into African markets, agricultural projects related to people's livelihood, resource development, and industrial (economic and trade) parks.

In addition to these policy banks, China's Ministry of Commerce, which houses the department of foreign aid, oversees projects financed through zero-interest loans (and grants) and signs off on Exim Bank's concessional loans (Brautigam and Hwang, 2016). Moreover, commercial banks such as the China Construction Bank, the Bank of China and the Industrial and Commercial Bank of China (ICBC) are also active in Africa supporting trade and construction tenders (Brautigam and Hwang, 2016).

China provides eight categories of foreign assistance to African countries: funding for complete projects, goods and materials, technical cooperation, human resource development cooperation, medical assistance, emergency humanitarian aid, volunteer programs and debt relief. The assistance benefits different sectors such as health care, agriculture, education, transportation, energy and communications. Many of the projects supported within these sectors (especially in transport and energy) require large investment and long pay-back terms that traditional donors are reluctant to provide (Degele and Seshagiri, 2019). Overall, between 2000 and 2014 China provided roughly

Table 9 Chinese financial institutions lending funds to Africa, 2000–2014

Lender	Amount (US $bn)	Percentage of total finance
China Export-Import (EXIM) Bank	$59.00	68.45
China Development Bank	$13.70	15.89
Company Suppliers' Credit	$7.70	8.93
Industrial Commercial Bank of China (ICBC)	$3.30	3.83
Ministry of Commerce and other	$2.50	2.9
Total	$86.20	100

Source: Table 1 in Brautigam and Hwang (2016)

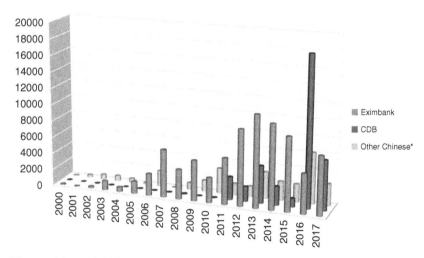

Figure 6 Annual Chinese loans to African governments by lender, 2000–2017 (US$mn) **Note:** *Includes commercial Chinese banks and Chinese contractors. **Source:** SAISI-CARI Loan database

$86.2 billion to African governments and other state-owned enterprises (Brautigam and Hwang, 2016). These finances were largely loan based and financed by the Chinese government's financial institutions, with the biggest financier being Exim Bank, followed by the CDB (Table 9 and Figure 6). The Ministry of Commerce also provides a small amount of interest-free loans, grants and in-kind aid (Brautigam and Hwang, 2016).

Chinese finances are disbursed across various sectors in Africa (Brautigam and Hwang, 2014; Sun, 2014) but the majority of that funding goes to infrastructure (transportation, energy, and communications) and natural resources (mining). A large proportion (more than 83 percent) of the funds disbursed to mining benefits resource-rich countries (Angola, oil; Ivory Coast and Eritrea, gold; Niger, uranium; Democratic Republic of Congo, copper; Morocco, geochemical mapping project) (Brautigam and Hwang, 2016).

2.2.2 Investment

In spite of the skepticism and criticism of China's motives in Africa, evidence suggests that China is there for the long haul because of its willingness to invest in Africa's infrastructure. It is well known that infrastructure (transportation, energy, information and communications technology and water) is essential for raising productivity in both the formal and informal sectors, and infrastructure projects are the most profitable investments a country can make (AfDB, 2018). China also facilitates trade by enabling export-oriented firms to access international markets quickly, cheaply and efficiently, and underpins the competitiveness of both the manufacturing and agricultural sectors (AfDB, 2018). Yet Africa as a whole has insufficient stock of productive infrastructure in power, water and transportation services, which is retarding its industrialization efforts (AfDB, 2018). In fact, the African Development Bank (AfDB) estimates that currently the continent has an annual infrastructure need of around $130–170 billion, with a financing gap of $68–108 billion (AfDB, 2018, Deloitte, 2016). This is despite the concerted efforts African countries have made so far in investing roughly $324 billion in infrastructure projects (AfDB, 2018).

China, unlike traditional donors, presents a unique opportunity for investing in Africa's infrastructure sector through its Belt and Road Initiative (BRI) (Chen and Lin, 2018). The BRI – also known as One Belt, One Road or the Silk Road Economic Belt and the twenty-first-century maritime Silk Road – is a centerpiece of President Xi Jinping's foreign economic policy. It includes a network of roads, railroads, ports and maritime infrastructure linking China to Central and South Asia and Europe and to the new maritime Silk Road linking China to Southeast Asia, East Africa, North Africa, the Gulf countries and Europe. In the case of Africa, it provides the opportunity to accelerate infrastructure development, regional integration and industrial development (Chen and Lin, 2018).

Djibouti has emerged as Africa's BRI hub in addition to being the location of China's first overseas naval facility. As a result, it has benefited from China's funding in the amount of $1.8 billion for the construction of multiple infrastructure projects including the $590 million, 690 hectare Doraleh multipurpose port and a free trade zone complex cofinanced by the Djibouti Ports and Free Zones

Authority (DPFZA) and China Merchant Holding (CMHC) [Africanews, 2017; Chen and Lin, 2018; Kiganda, 2017]. While BRI in Africa is still in the early stages with the majority of the activities in eastern Africa, there are notable projects in countries such as Kenya and Ethiopia. For example, China funded a $3.4 billion electrified standard-gauge railway (SGR) connecting Addis Ababa in Ethiopia and the port of Djibouti and a $5.3 billion SGR connecting the cities of Mombasa and Nairobi in Kenya. In addition Kenya has secured a total of $7 billion (financed in stages) to construct another SGR from Nairobi to Malaba (a border town between Kenya and Uganda) via Kisumu (Kacungira, 2017; Kagera, 2017; Mbogo, 2018; Ngugi, 2017; Raballa, 2017). The Nairobi-Malaba SGR is currently under construction and is expected to connect to other SGRs in Uganda, Rwanda, Burundi, South Sudan and eastern Democratic Republic of the Congo under the East African Railway Master Plan (Moore, 2014). Other BRI projects in the works are the deepwater port in Lamu, Kenya and the Lamu-Port-South Sudan – Ethiopia Transport (LAPSSET) corridor connecting Kenya, South Sudan and Ethiopia (Kazungu, 2018; Sisay, 2019). Plans are also under way to construct an SGR in Tanzania that will connect Dar es Salaam to Rwanda (Tiezzi, 2018).

The BRI has ventured into digital infrastructure through an "information silk road" (Chen and Lin, 2018) as exemplified by the announcement in September 2017 of China Mobile International's (CMI) partnership with the Djibouti Data Center (DDC) to establish cable head access, cross-connect, colocation and undersea fiber cable access services in East Africa (Melick and Cheng, 2017; Techerati, 2017).[12] The objective of the projects is to facilitate China's global network expansion not only in Africa but also to other regional hubs in Asia and Europe.

Despite China's widely publicized investment in Africa's infrastructure sector, the biggest source of funding for infrastructure projects in many African countries is African governments (see Table 10; Deloitte, 2019), followed by International Development Association (IDA) member countries. However, at the country level China is the biggest donor, providing more than Arab countries and multilateral development banks (MDBs) and other bilateral donors combined. Between 2012 and 2016 African governments financed 30 percent of the infrastructure budget, while IDA countries provided 20 percent. China funded 12 percent of the budget; Arab countries, MDBs and other bilateral donors combined provided a total of 6.9 percent of the infrastructure funding budgetary needs.

---

[12] DDC is the first and currently the only Tier 3 carrier-neutral data center environment in East Africa with direct access to all major international and regional fiber-optic systems connecting Europe, the Middle East and Asia with Africa – including Asia-Africa-Europe 1 (AAE-1) and Southeast Asia-Middle East-Western Europe 5 (SeaMeWe-5) (Techerati, 2017).

Table 10 Trends in infrastructure finance in Africa by source (US$bn)

Source	2012	2013	2014	2015	2016	Average
African governments	26.3	30.5	43.6	24	26.3	**30.14**
Donors (IDA members)	18.7	25.3	18.8	19.8	18.6	**20.24**
MDBs and other bilateral donors	1.7	2	3.5	2.4	3.1	**2.54**
China	13.7	13.4	3.1	20.9	6.4	**11.5**
Arab countries	5.2	3.3	3.4	4.4	5.5	**4.36**
Private	9.5	8.8	2.9	7.4	2.6	**6.24**
Total	**75.1**	**83.3**	**75.3**	**78.9**	**62.5**	**75.02**

Source: AfDB (2018)

In many ways China has presented itself as a unique investor not only in Africa but also in other developing regions. Relative to OECD member countries, the Chinese government and entrepreneurs are willing to invest in risky projects and countries (Feng and Pilling, 2019). China was willing to invest in Sudan's oil fields and fund the Sudanese government when Western investors left due to the civil conflict. China has also had a strong presence in Angola, the Democratic Republic of Congo and Liberia despite the uncertainties in these countries associated with either corrupt governments or civil conflicts. Chinese entrepreneurs have invested in nearly every sector in Africa and have extended their investment activities to retail and street vending (Feng and Pilling, 2019; Shepard, 2019). In countries like Nigeria Chinese entrepreneurs own and operate free trade zones like small countries within a country, with their own customs systems and security:

> "It is like managing a country," Mr Wu says of the zone, which is designed to be an enclave of efficiency and stability in Nigeria's notoriously unpredictable business environment. "We have our own customs, our own police, our own operations. The government of Nigeria provided the land. We used all our own money to build everything else." After seven years in operation, the free trade zone has 50 registered companies, including two ceramic manufacturers producing tiles and plates, a steel-pipe plant and factories making everything from furniture to tomato sauce. There is a printing business, a plastic recycling company and another specializing in construction materials. (Feng and Pilling, 2019)

Chinese enterprises handle an estimated $500 billion of Africa's industrial output and the value of their businesses is currently around $2 trillion (Feng and Pilling, 2019; Shepard, 2019). More than 10,000 Chinese companies are estimated to be operating in Africa, with Nigeria and Zambia hosting 920 and 861, respectively, of those companies. The Chinese population in Africa is also growing, whereby roughly 1 million Chinese currently reside in different parts of Africa (French, 2014) as migrant labor and entrepreneurs (Park, 2016).

2.2.3 Debt Crises and Natural Resources Concerns

One of the major concerns about China's finance in Africa is the potential of plunging these countries (especially heavily indebted poor countries [HIPCs]) back into foreign debt that would reach beyond sustainable levels. Moreover, many economists believe that China's main motive is to access Africa's rich natural resources (Amusa, Monkam and Viegi, 2016; Shinn and Eisenman, 2012; Sun, 2014; Tull, 2006). In fact, some have categorically dubbed China an exploiter of the poor and a grabber of Africa's resources, which is contrary to China's Africa policy statement (in the 2006 white paper) of seeking "mutual benefit, reciprocity and common prosperity" (Mourdoukoutas, 2018; Shinn and Eisenman, 2012; Tull, 2006). At face value these concerns are valid, particularly because among the top ten African countries receiving Chinese financing (see Table 7A) seven are richly endowed with oil or ores and five are categorized as HIPCs (meaning that they are beneficiaries of the IMF-World Bank debt relief initiatives).

Indeed, about one-third of Chinese loans to Africa are backed by commodities or escrow accounts (Brautigam and Hwang, 2016). While the concern that China is trying to grab Africa's natural resource could be valid, evidence suggests that this model of financing has been in practice for quite some time largely for the purpose of hedging against risk when lending to poor or unstable countries that have little creditworthiness, but with assets that provide collateral in case of default (Brautigam and Hwang, 2016). At a country level, many financial institutions around the world have used agricultural output and other forms of inventory as collateral in lending (Coulter and Onumah, 2002; Hollinger, Rutten and Kiriakov, 2009; IFC, 2013; Varangis and Larson, 2002; Varangis, Saint-Geours and Albert, 2017; World Bank, 2016). Bilateral commodity-backed lending took place in the 1970s when Japan supported China's economic reconstruction in exchange for China's coal and oil (Brautigam and Hwang, 2016); a recent op-ed (Songwe, 2013) at the Brookings Institute suggests that the World Bank and the IMF could be considering this model of financing. Thus, China's current model of commodity-backed lending in Africa and other developing countries in Latin America and Asia is not new, and it worked for China in the 1970s. The question now remaining to be answered at some point in the future is whether this could lead to another wave of grabbing Africa's natural resources in the case of loan defaults or unfavorable changes in commodity prices.

Evidence abounds of China's commodity-backed lending in African countries (Table 11). Angola was the first country in Africa to receive large-scale commodity-backed lending, and so far it is the largest borrower of commodity-backed loans from China. This model has been extended to other countries on the continent. The commodities used include oil, ores and agricultural output (cocoa beans, sesame seeds). In other cases, loans and lines of credit have been backed by future profits and escrow accounts. For example, Ghana secured an electric power plant loan with future revenue from sales of electricity, while Kenya obtained its SGR loan through an escrow account of revenues from rail traffic (Brautigam and Hwang, 2016).

The possibility that China's finances in Africa could plunge vulnerable countries into unsustainable debt and strip them bare of their natural resources cannot be ignored. One area that raises such concerns is the terms of Chinese loans and lines of credit. As shown in Brautigam and Hwang (2016), a large portion of China's commodity-backed loans are at non-concessional rates based

Table 11 Chinese commodity-backed official lines of credit and loans for projects completed, 2000–2014

Year	Country	Amount (US$mn)	Purpose	Commodity
2001	Sudan	128	Gas power station	Oil
2002	Nigeria	115	Power plant	Oil
2003	Congo	238	Hydropower	Oil
2004	Angola	2,000	Multisector	Oil
2006	Nigeria	200	NICOMSAT satellite	Oil
2006	Zimbabwe	200	Farm equipment and materials	Platinum deposit
2007	Ghana	292	Hydropower	Cocoa and electricity offtake
2007	Angola	500	Multisector	Oil
2009	Sudan	86	Road	Oil
2009	Sudan	120	Road	Oil
2010	Angola	2,500	Kilamba Kiaxi city housing project	Oil
2010	Sudan	66	Bridge	Oil
2011	Zimbabwe	105	National Defense College	Diamond income in escrow account

Source: Tables 3 and 4 in Brautigam and Hwang (2016)

on the London interbank offer rate (libor) plus a margin (basis points). In some cases the basis points are much higher than what the country would have obtained from a non-Chinese lender [see Brautigam and Hwang, (2016) for the case of Angola]. Also, while the regular loans from China to African countries tend to have a lower interest rate and longer repayment period (compared to that extended to Latin American countries and loans from other bilateral and multilateral lenders), they are often tied to goods and services from China. This implies that the economic multiplier effects (from horizontal linkages) that could arise if all the money was spent directly in the recipient countries are curtailed. Such multiplier effects are important for wider economic growth and resulting tax revenues that could help the government repay the loan faster. Nonetheless, an assessment by Brautigam and Hwang (2016) suggests that most of these countries are not at risk of debt crises, at least for now.

2.3 Africa's Foreign Finance Policy in the Context of China's Finance

Africa is an agrarian society largely dependent on agriculture. Its population is about 1.2 billion, of which more than 400 million are youths in the age range of fifteen to thirty-five years. Since a large percentage of the African economy is in the informal sector, it is hard to gauge the true unemployment rate; however, according to International Labor Organization (ILO) data (ILO, 2018), only 34 percent of Africa's workers had wage-paying jobs or were employers in 2017, and 66 percent were in vulnerable employment as own-account or family workers. Moreover, both poverty and illiteracy rates are high, with about 35 percent of the population living in extreme poverty (based on 2013 estimate, OECD [2018]), and adult literacy rates in SSA are estimated at 60 percent [2010 estimates, based on World Development Indicators (WDI) database].

These facts suggest that Africa needs to expand its formal sector by growing the industry sector (particularly the manufacturing subsector), which not only boosts the economy through increasing the value chain but also creates better-paying, more secure jobs, and increases employment opportunities, especially for the low-skilled labor force. This can be achieved by attracting labor-intensive foreign direct investment and expanding the tradable sector by increasing the goods and services exported, diversifying the export basket and expanding the number of trading partners. Indeed, Africa has made some progress in diversifying the number of trade partners (especially with China, India and other emerging economies) and increasing its trade volume from $276 billion in 2000 to $806 billion in 2016 (OECD, 2018). However, Africa continues to export raw material (primary products) and import manufactured products (see Figure 7). It has not demonstrated any clear strategy to expand its manufacturing subsector, especially in its relation with China, which is now Africa's largest trading partner.

Similar to experiences in developed countries, most African producers cannot compete effectively with Chinese companies even in Africa's own domestic markets as they cannot undercut Chinese production costs and prices. Local retailers face rapidly increasing business competition from expatriate Chinese traders that has extended to the informal sector, specifically street vending. Yet China has positioned itself as a country that can help Africa on the basis of mutual benefit. But the relationship between China and Africa is clearly asymmetric, especially in trade and job creation (Shinn and Eisenman, 2012; Tull, 2006). Moreover, the use of imported personnel and intermediate material by Chinese companies is unlikely to help build local industries and transfer technologies (Alden, 2006) as suggested in China's guiding principles of its engagement with Africa.

However, as expected, China's goal, like that of any rational economic player or political strategist, is to act in the best interest of its people. Unfortunately, Africa has always had the mentality of expecting other countries and players to act in altruistic ways that benefit its economies and people instead of taking a more proactive, forward-looking and logical economic stance that looks out for its own interests in all circumstances. It expects China to play a lead rather

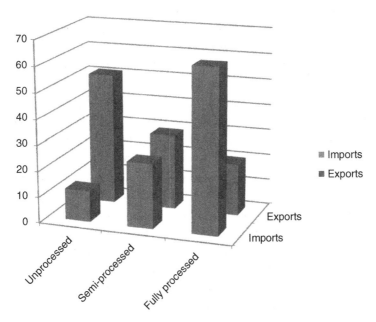

Figure 7 Trade composition in Africa, 2016
Source: Figure 1.2. in OECD (2018)

than a supporting role, contrary to economic principles. Africa presents itself as a guest even in its own backyard, while China and other players play the host, and in due course, allows others to dictate the rules and pace of its economic development. According to Osakwe (2017), the responsibility of Africa's development should rest primarily with African governments, and it is upon African policy makers to put forth policies that ensure Africa's development needs and challenges are effectively met.

There is little doubt that natural resources are at the core of China's economic interest in Africa (Tull, 2006). Undoubtedly Africa has the most sought-after crude oil because of its quality (it is light), and there are very few places in the world with high probabilities of significant new oil and gas discoveries except in Africa (Lee and Shalmon, 2008). For these reasons China is willing to go to great lengths to access Africa's oil (Lee and Shalmon, 2008) and other ores and minerals for its massive industry sector and to obtain a favored status (Lee and Shalmon, 2008). African leaders should recognize this and use their enormous wealth to gain an upper hand when negotiating for loans, grants and trade deals. For example, they should require that instead of exporting crude oil, interested companies and countries should build refineries in the country to spur employment in local communities. Also, extracted mineral and ores should be equally processed in the country and exported as final products. However, very few countries have attempted to make this requirement, and China has quickly shunned those that have tried (like Angola in 2006).

Experiences with Western donors and multinational companies should have prepared African leaders and policy makers to preemptively put in place – in the early stages of their partnership with China – guidelines that govern the flow of foreign aid, trade, investment and other aspects of economic interactions to ensure that Africa's interests are well served. For example, similar to China's FOCAC (a coordinating body for China's engagement with African countries), African leaders through the African Union should put forth a counterpart body or committee to guide such engagements. By the same measures that China has many policy papers that clearly spell out its guiding principles on foreign engagement, especially with African countries, the African Union should have a working Africa-China policy paper to stipulate its engagements with China. So far, such a paper does not exist, at least in the public domain.

As noted in Rotberg (2008), neither the African Union nor the subregional organizations have an articulated policy regarding Chinese influence in Africa. Instead, each of the countries is responding to China idiosyncratically, employing the same failed strategy used with Western countries, international financial institutions and multinational enterprises. This raises the question of whether African countries have learned (or are willing to learn) any lessons from past mistakes where they have often assumed the follower role at the expense of their natural resources and economic growth and development. It is not too late to change course. Africa as a continent should develop bold, specific and effective policies toward China (and other donors) that welcome foreign investment and trade, but condemn exporting to African markets substandard goods and services, taking away African jobs, practicing poor labor standards, destroying African industries and exploiting Africa's natural resources. As stated in Rotberg (2008: 18):

> Without concerted African ground rules and improved governance at home, China will continue to be opportunistic, exploiting weaker nation-states in its quest for resources and asserting its own overweening economic leverage with little consideration for African values and (development) needs. African countries need to try and meet China half-way if they are to stand on equal footing with China. They need to join forces and channel Chinese energies and capital in directions that benefit Africa as much as they benefit China. Only by fashioning such a collective response can African (countries) throughout the continent turn China's massive and multifaceted drive into Africa to their sustainable best advantage.

Ample examples highlight the urgent need for African countries to develop a policy paper on foreign finances, especially with China. Particularly, contrary to the rosy image painted in the eight principles that Premier Enlai outlined during his speech in Ghana and Mali in 1964, and in the 2006 white paper on "China's African Policy," many observers and researchers have remarked that Africa is relieving with China the typical bona fide colonial economic relationship that characterized its interactions with the Europeans and North Americans and that contributed to Africa's asymmetrical integration into global markets (*The Economist, 2004*). For example:

1. Data show that nearly all projects (including infrastructure projects) funded by Chinese loans or grants are implemented by Chinese companies. Moreover, a large percentage of the materials used in these projects is imported from China.
2. The labor employed to work on the Chinese-funded projects, from management to unskilled labor, is imported from China (Alden 2006; Lee and Shalmon, 2008).
3. Chinese workers who travel to Africa tend to get special treatment; living in their own enclaves, they do not attempt to learn the local language, their children go to Chinese schools, they eat in Chinese restaurants, and they import nearly everything they need from China. They therefore have very minimal interaction with and contribution to the local community (Lee and Shalmon, 2008).

4. Currently China imports cheap raw material from Africa and exports expensive processed manufactured goods to Africa, with the trade balance highly in China's favor. While China trades with all fifty-four African countries, 71 percent of its imports from the continent are from only four countries (Angola, Libya, South Africa and Sudan), and 84 percent of those imports are natural resources (Wang and Elliot, 2014).

5. In 2006 Angola tried to persuade Sinopec to build a 240,000 bbl/d refinery in Lobito. The negotiations collapsed because of differences about the target market (Angola preferred Africa while Sinopec preferred China) and because Sinopec's preference was to build a refinery in China rather than Angola.

3 Case Study: Tanzania

3.1 Tanzania's Macroeconomic Structure

Tanzania is largely an agrarian society. A large percentage (about 73 percent during the 2000–2017 period) of its population lives in rural communities where the poverty level is relatively high. In 2012 the rural poverty rate was about 33 percent compared to the national rate of 28 percent (World Bank, 2015). Infrastructure development (such as roads, access to clean water, improved sanitation and electricity, and social infrastructure [including hospitals and schools]) is very low by international standards and in comparison to neighboring countries. While a large percentage of the population works in the informal sector, the employment rate in the formal sector is around 80 percent. A large proportion of this employment is in the agricultural sector (72 percent between 2000 and 2017), reflective of the rural-urban population distribution. The services sector is the second largest employer, accounting for roughly 22 percent of the total employment in the 2000–2017 period. Employment in the industry sector is very minimal (5.3 percent in the 2000–2017 period), suggestive of the low level of industrialization of Tanzania's economy. In terms of volume of trade and export diversification, 50 percent of Tanzania's GDP is due to trade (1990–2012), which is composed of largely primary sector products as demonstrated by the low export concentration[13] and high export diversification[14] indices that averaged 0.27 and 0.78, respectively, between 2000 and 2017 (see Figure 8).

---

[13] An export concentration index shows the degree to which a country is dependent on exports. A concentration close to zero suggests that a country is more dependent on exports (Wamboye and Mookerjee, 2014).

[14] An export diversification index measures the depth of a country's export basket. A country whose exports consist of a large number of products and that trades with several other countries has a lower export diversification index (Wamboye and Mookerjee, 2014).

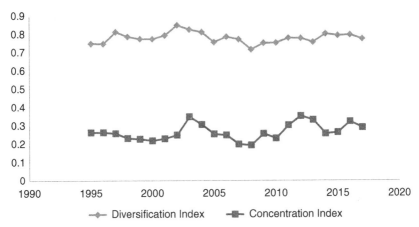

Figure 8 Tanzania's export diversification and concentration indices, 2000–2017
Source: Author's calculations based on UNCTAD database

The Tanzanian government relies (to a significant extent) on foreign assistance for budgetary support. During the 2017/2018 fiscal year, roughly 13 percent of the budget was financed by grants and concessional loans (including general budget support, project loans and grants and basket loans and grants [Ministry of Finance and Planning (MoFP), 2018]. Moreover, 24.5 percent of the budget revenues were from external non-concessional borrowing (MoFP, 2018). In terms of the 2017/2018 development budget, 25 percent of the funds were from foreign sources (MoFP, 2018). This foreign dependency has real consequences for the ability of the government to carry out its development agenda because of delays in accessing the loans and grants (MoFP, 2019). For instance, as of April 2018, only 26 percent of the foreign funds allocated to the development budget (in the 2017/2018 fiscal year) had been released (MoFP, 2019).

Furthermore, Tanzania is one of the thirty-three countries in Africa categorized as least developed by the United Nations, implying that it is among the poorest countries in the world. The category of least developed countries (LDCs) was established in 1971 and Tanzania has been on that list since. Despite the international community's recognition and preferential treatment of LDCs, no country has ever graduated from this group, an indication that the macroeconomic conditions that qualified them in the first place have not improved. It is surprising and ironic that a number of LDCs (e.g. Angola, the Central African Republic, the Democratic Republic of Congo, Mozambique, Sierra Leone, South Sudan and Tanzania) are highly endowed with natural resources, including oil and ores.

Evidence shows that Tanzania is the third largest ODA recipient in Africa, after Ethiopia and the Democratic Republic of Congo (AfDB, 2017; Stewart,

2013). Between 2000 and 2017 Tanzania received a total of $40.5 billion in net ODA and official aid (constant 2015 US dollars). The trend shows a steady increase since 2000 (Figure 9) with an average increase of $2.3 billion annually.

Also as an HIPC, Tanzania has benefited from the IMF-World Bank HIPC debt relief initiatives and multilateral debt relief initiative (MDRI), which helped to expand its fiscal space for development programs. As of 2017, the share of Tanzania's external debt stock in gross national income (GNI) was 35 percent. Overall, Tanzania's external debt stock has reduced significantly from 166 percent of GNI in 1994 and 71 percent in 2000 to 22 percent in 2008 (the lowest level) (see Figure 10). Equally, the share of the country's debt service in exports of goods, services and primary income (which measures a country's ability to service its external debt) declined from 18 percent in 1994 to 11 percent in 2000 and down to 0.6 percent in 2008 (the lowest level). In 2017, the share of debt service in exports was about 6.5 percent. Note that Tanzania reached its decision point in April 2000 and completion point in November 2001, two of the required steps a country must complete in order to receive full and irrevocable reduction in debt under the HIPC debt relief initiative. This implies that by November 2001, after reaching the completion point, Tanzania's debt owed to the IMF and other external creditors was significantly reduced, consistent with what is observed in the data (see Figure 10).

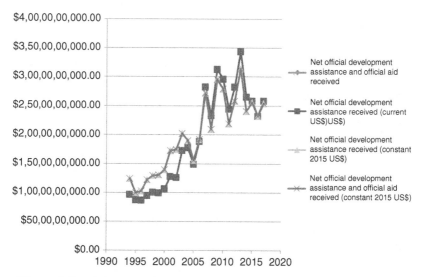

Figure 9 Trends in Tanzania's official development assistance and official aid received (1994–2017)
Source: Author's calculations based on WDI online dataset, 2019

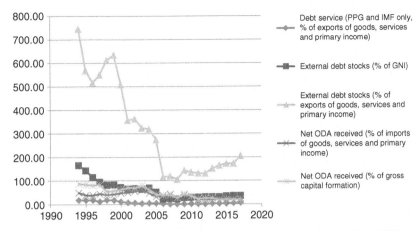

Figure 10 Trends in Tanzania's debt stock and debt services, 1994–2017
Source: Author's calculations based on WDI online dataset, 2019

Despite this seemingly bleak picture, Tanzania has made significant macro-economic improvements reflected in its consistently high economic growth rate of about 6.7 percent in the past eighteen years and its low inflation rate (as measured by GDP deflator) that averaged 7.6 percent between 2002 and 2017. Particularly, the government has made efforts to reduce the public sector payroll while increasing investment in heavy infrastructure (roads, railways and ports). With recent debt forgiveness through the HIPCs initiative and enhanced MDRI, Tanzania's public debt is at manageable levels with the share of external debt stock in GNI averaging 35 percent in the 2000–2017 period (see Figure 10). Another notable step the government has taken is to increase its fiscal space by improving tax revenue collection and tackling corruption and tax evasion. However, it is fair to mention that the aggressiveness of the tax collection has had short-run negative impacts on small and medium businesses by imposing liquidity constraint, in turn potentially curtailing their expansion and growth. The trade deficit has also narrowed, although it is expected to widen as the government increases its spending on infrastructure.

3.1.1 China's Finances in Tanzania

China has taken a very proactive role as Tanzania's bilateral development partner. Between 2000 and 2017 China loaned Tanzania roughly $2.64 billion (unadjusted US dollars), which was much smaller compared to its neighbors such as Ethiopia ($13.796 billion), Kenya ($8.9 billion), Zambia ($8.634 billion) and Malawi ($3.181 billion) (see Figure 11) that have received more loans. The majority (about 55 percent) of these loans (as it is everywhere in Africa) are

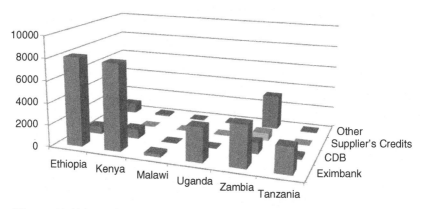

Figure 11 Chinese loans to Tanzania and neighboring countries, 2000–2017
(millions of US$, unadjusted)

Note: "Other" includes commercial Chinese banks and Chinese contractors.
Source: SAISI-CARI Loan database

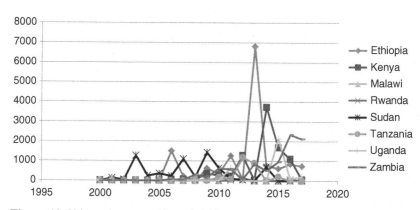

Figure 12 Chinese loans to selected African countries, 2000–2017 (millions of
US$, unadjusted)
Source: SAISI-CARI Loan database

funded by China's Exim Bank. The bulk of these loans was received between
2008 and 2015. As shown in Figure 12, China started providing a noticeable
amount of loans and other financial flows to African countries around 2006 (with
the exception of Sudan), six years after the first FOCAC conference.

A research lab at the College of William and Mary (USA) known as AIDDATA
compiles a database that details information on all forms of financial flows from
China to African countries. The database includes not only the amount disbursed
but also the sector and projects that benefited from those amounts. We take

Table 12 Sectoral distribution of Chinese finance in Tanzania, 2000–2014

Sector	Number of funded projects	Number of unfunded projects	Amount (2014 US dollars)	Share of total (percent)
Debt forgiveness	6	0	$257,813,829.00	1.10
Agriculture, forestry and fishing	3	4	$16,383,070.00	0.07
Communications	133	6	$14,659,018,580.00	62.59
Developmental food aid/food security assistance	1	0	$1,807,233.00	0.01
Education	6	13	$1,898,847.00	0.01
Emergency response	1	0	$18,138.00	0.00
Nonfood commodity assistance	0	1	$0.00	0.00
Government and civil society	10	2	$259,461,662.00	1.11
Health	5	52	$18,775,709.00	0.08
Industry, mining, construction	5	0	$6,486,592,040.00	27.70
Other multisector	2	1	$250,695.00	0.00
Other social infrastructure and services	6	4	$131,651,280.00	0.56
Transport and storage	7	1	$1,046,732,871.00	4.47
Water supply and sanitation	36	4	$539,318,350.00	2.30
Women in development	1	1	$5,082.00	0.00
Total	222	89	$23,419,727,386.00	100.00

Source: Author's calculations based on AidData database

advantage of this database to provide the nuances of China's engagement in Tanzania. As summarized in Table 12, China funded 222 projects and provided eighty-nine in-kind services or pieces of equipment to Tanzania between 2000 and 2014 (the latest year for which data are available). The funded projects were equivalent to $23.4 billion (in 2014 US dollars). The projects were in a variety of sectors, with the top four being communications, industry, mining and construction, transport and storage, and water supply and sanitation. In fact, during the 2000–2014 period, these four sectors alone accounted for roughly 97 percent of China's finance (grants and loans) in Tanzania. Communications, a subsector of the services sector, attracted the largest number of funded projects (133), which was equivalent to 63 percent ($14.6 billion in 2014 US dollars) of the total Chinese finance in Tanzania during the 2000–2014 period. The second sector was industry, mining and construction with five funded projects in the amount of $6.5 billion (27.7 percent). Transportation and storage came in third place with seven funded projects costing $1.04 billion (4.47 percent). Water supply and sanitation was the fourth highest-funded sector, receiving 2.3 percent of total financing within the 2000–2014 period, equivalent to $539.3 million (in 2014 US dollars). Other sectors that received considerable amounts were government and civil society ($259.5 million) with ten funded projects, and other social infrastructure ($131.7 million) with six funded projects). Tanzania also received debt forgiveness in the amount of $257.8 million.

While aggregation is important in providing an overview of the sectors funded, and the amount allocated to each sector, information that is more useful for policy formulation lies in the disaggregate data where we can evaluate the types of projects, the amount each of these projects received, the funding and implementing agencies and where (city/region) the project was implemented. Such information helps us to understand where the Chinese interest lies in Tanzania, and thus China's financing policy in the country. In the sections that follow we look at each of these key sectors in detail.

Information and Communication Technologies (ICTs) Sector

Infrastructure projects are among the most profitable investments in any country. They reduce transaction costs, increase productivity and drive economic growth by increasing the efficiency of the core sectors (agriculture, industry and service) of the economy (AfDB, 2018). One category of infrastructure that took Africa by storm and transformed the continent is information and communication technologies (ICTs). This is a continent where by 2000 the penetration of landline telephones (especially in SSA) was less than 1 percent. The common technology of information dissemination was radio and print newspapers (largely in big cities), and a large percentage of the population relied on word of mouth as a means of passing and gathering information. However, the introduction of cellphones and, later, internet access has transformed every facet of the economy and sector from e-banking, e-health and e-government to the introduction of business process outsourcing (BPO) and revolutionizing the labor market and political institutions with noticeable impact on governance, economic growth and development.

These ICTs have defined the future of Africa in a way that the world had not envisioned and have set the need for other infrastructure in power/energy, transport, water and sanitation. The most noticeable impact of ICTs is how they have made the countries on the continent realize the transformative power of infrastructure. In fact, most of the countries on the continent now have an infrastructure development component in their development plans.

The AfDB has developed Africa's infrastructure development index (AIDI) that ranks African countries on the basis of their readiness in meeting infrastructure needs for development. The index has four components of infrastructure (transport, electricity, ICTs and water and sanitation) and ranges from 0 to 100 with a higher value indicating more readiness. Recent (2013–2016) data show that Seychelles has consistently ranked higher among African countries with values of 84.41 (2013) and 93.92 (2016). The top ten countries over these four years were consistently from North and southern Africa. Countries in West and East Africa have indices less than 30 with most of them in the lower teens. Other nations like Somalia, South Sudan and Niger have indices in the single digits. Tanzania ranked between 43 (2016) and 45 (2013) over these four years with the index ranging between 10.21 and 11.97 (2016). This shows that Tanzania, like many of the countries in Africa, is not close to meeting its infrastructure needs (AfDB, 2017).

Data for the specific components show that the ICT sector has been the main driver of improvements in the AIDI over the past decade. According to the AfDB (2015) report "African Telecom Infrastructure Investment Needs," 2005–2010 was a period of very high growth for mobile telephony, marked by the emergence of new operators in the market and by massive growth in coverage extensions and broadband speeds, as well as user subscriptions. The 2010–2015 period also witnessed the installation of new submarine cables, which provided huge new capacity around countries along the coast, as well as facilitating the consolidation of mobile telephony operators. Tanzania is one of those countries that have had a noticeable improvement in its ICTs composite index compared to the other three components of AIDI, thus improving its overall index and ranking. Particularly between 2000 and 2015, the country saw accelerated progress in wired broadband internet subscriptions (AfDB, 2016). These changes are reflected in the ICTs composite index as well. For example, there was a 50 percent and 48 percent increase in the index value from 2013 to 2014, and 2014 to 2015, respectively.

As indicated previously, one of the top five sectors that benefit from China's finance in Africa is the ICT sector. In Tanzania, it is also the sector that received the largest share of the funds that China disbursed to the country between 2000 and 2014. It is not surprising that this sector is one of Tanzania's five fastest-growing sectors (MoFP, 2016). In 2017, the sector grew by 14.7 percent, surpassed only by mining and quarrying (17.5 percent), water supply (16.7 percent) and transport and storage (16.6 percent). The growth was largely on account of expansion of the use of mobile phone services, an increase in airtime sales and expansion of broadband and internet services. The sector's contribution to Tanzania's GDP in 2017 and 2016 was 2 percent, ranking fourteenth in terms of its importance in the country's GDP (MoFP, 2018).

China has undoubtedly contributed to the success of the ICT sector in Tanzania. As shown in Table 12, China funded 133 projects in this sector equivalent to $14,6459,018,580 (in 2014 US dollars). The funding took place between 2008 and 2013 for the purpose of development. All the projects were funded by Exim Bank and implemented by two Chinese state-owned companies (International Telecommunication Construction Corporation [ITCC] and the China Communications Construction Company [CCCC]) in different regions of the country. Eighty-seven of the 133 disbursements were made in 2008 in equal amounts of $9,652,3917 (in 2014 US dollars) and 45 of them were disbursed in 2010 in the amounts of $130,037,471 (in 2014 US dollars), with one last disbursement ($409,751,606 [in 2014 US dollars]) in 2013. The first eighty-seven projects consisted of building the national fiber-optic backbone phase one in different regions of the country, and the second forty-five projects involved building the national ICT broad infrastructure project phase two. The last project funded in 2013 was related to building the national ICT broad infrastructure project phase three.

In addition, between 2012 and 2013 China provided six in-kind donations/services to Tanzania of unspecified amounts. Five of them were categorized as grants, while one was free-standing technical assistance. For example, in 2012 China provided training for broadcasting technical staff in Zanzibar, while in 2013 China donated five television broadcast trucks to Tanzanian broadcasting corporations for the Mtwara, Tanga, Zanzibar, and Bagamoyo regions.

The construction of the first phase (7,000 km) of Tanzania's 10,674 km national fiber-optic backbone that began in February 2009 was completed in May 2010, connecting Dar es Salaam with towns and cities in northern and western Tanzania, and with neighboring Burundi, Rwanda, Kenya and Uganda. This phase covered three routes: northern ring 1 (Babati, Arusha, Moshi and Tanga), northern ring 2 (Dar es Salaam, Morogoro, Iringa, Dodoma and Singida) and western rings 1 and 2 (Shinyanga, Mwanza, Geita, Biharamulo, Rusumo and Kabanga) (Sedoyeka and Sicilima, 2016).

The completion of phase one fiber-optic network closed a significant gap in the East African ring connecting the SEACOM, TEAMS and EASSY submarine cables and running from Mombasa (Kenya) and through Nairobi (Kenya), Kampala (Uganda), Kigali (Rwanda), Bujumbura (Burundi) to Dar es Salaam (Tanzania). The second phase connects the southern and eastern towns and cities of Tanzania to the neighboring countries of Zambia and Malawi.

Industry and Mining Sector

The first project funded in the industry and mining sector in Tanzania was the Kiwira Coal Mine in 2007, which was classified as an official investment for commercial purposes. It received $542,568,220.9 (in 2011 US dollars). The Kiwira Coal Mine was constructed by the Chinese at the invitation of the late president Julius Nyerere. Construction began in 1982 and commissioning in 1988. The Chinese remained at the mine to manage operations until 1997 when management was transferred to the Tanzanian government (Binala, 2018). However, ten years later the mines were closed due to mismanagement. Before and after the closure, the mine went through a series of name and management changes without noticeable changes in revenues and productivity. In 2005 Kiwira Coal Mines Limited was privatized to a local company, Tan Power Resources Limited (TPR) with an objective of increasing production to 200 megawatts of energy (Binala, 2018). TPR acquired 70 percent of the shareholding while the government through Consolidated Holding Corporation (CHC) retained 30 percent. The name of the company was changed from Kiwira Coal Mines Limited to Kiwira Coal and Power Limited (KCPL). In 2008 the government decided to re-own the mine and in 2013 it handed the mine over to State Mining Corporation with the mandate to redevelop the mine and increase power generation (Binala, 2018). In 2012 a news report in *S&P Global* showed that the Chinese government had showed interest in investing $400 million to rehabilitate and operate the coal mine that will generate 200 megawatts of electricity for the national grid, according to the Ministry of Energy and Minerals (Matsiko, 2012).

The second project funded was the construction of a 535 kilometer Mtwara-Dar es Salaam gas pipeline with six funding disbursements. The first disbursement was in the amount of $1,170,305,616. The intention of this funding was developmental rather than commercial. The next five disbursements were of equal amounts of $1,297,318,408 (in 2014 US dollars). The disbursements were to fund the project in four regions: Pwani, Lindi, Mtwara and Dar es Salaam (two disbursements). The construction, which started in June 2013 under the management of the China Petroleum Technology and Development Corporation (CPTDC) (a subsidiary of the China National Petroleum

Company [CNPC]) and was completed in 2015, involved laying down pipeline (24–36 inches in diameter) from Mnazi Bay in Mtwara to Kinyerezi in Dar es Salaam via Somanga Fungu where there was already a spur line from the Songo-Songo gas field in Lindi (Xinhua, 2015). Other projects have been announced to build pipelines from Dar es Salaam to Bagamoyo (Dausen, 2019), and to build a refined products pipeline to transport petroleum from the port of Dar es Salaam to Zambia at a cost of $1.5 billion (Obulutsa, 2019).

Before the aforementioned extensions and improvements, Tanzania had three major pipelines by 2013, all of which serve the energy sector (AfDB, 2014). They are the TAZAMA pipeline that transports crude oil from the Dar es Salaam port to an oil refinery at Ndola in Zambia over a distance of 1,710 kilometers, the Songo-Songo pipeline that transfers natural gas from Songo-Songo Island to Dar es Salaam over a distance of 232 kilometers and the Mnazi Bay pipeline that transfers natural gas from the Mnazi gas field to a power plant in Mtwara over a distance of 28 kilometers.

Transport and Storage Sector

The transportation system consists of five components: road, air, rail, water and pipeline. Tanzania's road and air infrastructure performs well relative to that in other African countries, but the quality and distribution is below international standards (PWC, 2014). This negatively impacts productivity and growth. The rail and road network in the country has improved in the past three years, thanks in part to the Chinese funding. Tanzania currently has a road network of 86,472 kilometers as documented in the formal inventory, of which 12,786 kilometers are categorized as trunk roads, 21,105 kilometers as regional roads and the remaining 52,581 kilometers as district, urban and feeder roads (AfDB, 2014). Some of the roads are in poor condition due to many years of neglect and poor maintenance and a number of them are narrow with one lane, making them susceptible to adverse weather conditions and traffic congestion. The connectivity in rural areas is low, hampering the growth of the country's agriculture and mining sectors (PWC, 2014).

The rail system in Tanzania has two major lines (see Figure 13): the central line that runs from the economic capital, Dar es Salaam, to Tabora with branches to Kigoma and Tabora to Mwanza, and the Ruvu-Korogwe line, which has connections to the Tanga port and Moshi. Some parts of the rail system are not functioning due to poor maintenance, but the government has plans to rehabilitate and upgrade the entire rail system. In November 2012 Tanzania and China signed a $42 million agreement to rehabilitate the Tanzania-Zambia rail network (*African Review, 2012*).

Tanzania's port system is underdeveloped, limiting the country's ability to fully benefit from international trade. The port of Dar es Salaam is a major regional maritime hub, serving the neighboring landlocked countries of Rwanda, Uganda, the Democratic Republic of Congo, Malawi, Zambia and Burundi. However, despite this enormous trade potential and regional importance, the port faces steep competition from Kenya's Mombasa port, which is the largest port in East Africa. Currently the Dar es Salaam port handles 4.1 million tons of dry cargo and 6 million tons of bulk liquid cargo annually (PWC, 2014). While the port of Dar es Salaam ranks well in terms of container dwell time and crane productivity, the shipping costs to the port are among the highest in the world at 24 percent higher than the costs at other port facilities in SSA (PWC, 2014). The high costs can be attributed to delays in cargo handling arising from capacity constraints, which in turn are caused by poor backward linkages with inland transport networks and high traffic growth (PWC, 2014).

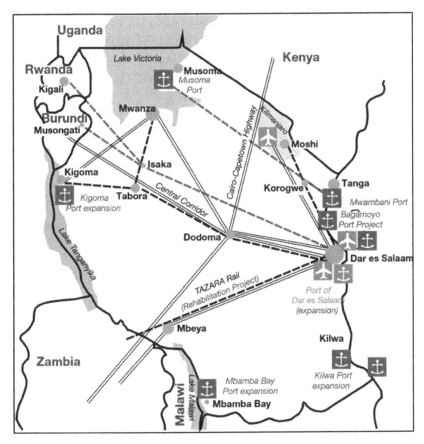

Figure 13 Tanzania's transport network

The Tanzania mainland has a total of fifty-eight airports managed by the Tanzanian airports authority, two of which are international airports (in Dar es Salaam and Arusha), with the Dar es Salaam airport receiving the highest traffic (AfDB, 2014). The island of Zanzibar also has an international airport. While all three international airports have seen some form of upgrading or expansion, they are currently operating beyond their designed capacity, especially Julius Nyerere International Airport in Dar es Salaam. In fact, Tanzania has one of the smallest international air markets in SSA. The country has other smaller airports that serve the domestic market (see Figure 13).

In reference to the Chinese finances, a total of seven projects were funded in the amount of $1,046,732,871 (in 2014 US dollars), making transport and storage the third largest beneficiary of Chinese funding in Tanzania, but the sector's funding dwarfed in comparison to Chinese financing of the same sector in neighboring Ethiopia and Kenya (see Figure 14). These projects were exclusively for air transportation infrastructure and were funded as loans for development purposes by Exim Bank and implemented by the state-owned Beijing Construction Engineering Company (BCEG). Specifically, in 2010 China gave two loans in equal amounts of $89,354,319 (in 2014 US dollars) to upgrade Abeid Amani Karume International Airport Terminal 2. In 2011 and 2013 China disbursed four additional loans – one in 2011 ($70 million in 2014

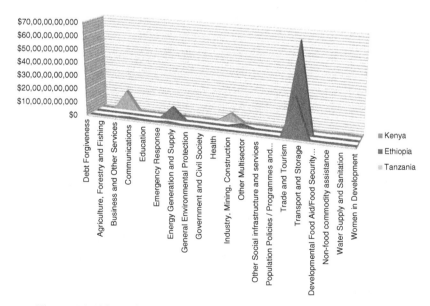

Figure 14 China's financial support to Kenya, Ethiopia and Tanzania, 2000–2014 (US$)
Source: SAISI-CARI Loan database

US dollars) and three of equal amounts in 2013 ($73.85 million/disbursement) – all for the purpose of upgrading/expanding Karume Airport.

Aside from the Chinese finances, Tanzania has been able to upgrade or expand other big infrastructure projects using internally sourced funds. In 2019 President Magufuli inaugurated a new state-of-the-art Terminal 3 at Julius Nyerere International Airport at a cost of $314 million (TSH 722 billion) (Xinhua, 2019). Terminals 1 and 2 at the same airport had also been upgraded using funds sourced domestically and loans from the Netherlands and China (Edwin, 2010). Other ongoing megaprojects financed by internal funds include the construction of the Rufiji hydropower plant expected to generate 2,115 megawatts, the upgrading and renovation of fifteen airports, the building of an SGR connecting the port of Dar es Salaam to the neighboring countries of Rwanda, Burundi and the Democratic Republic of Congo and the longest bridge over Lake Victoria and a number of road constructions (Dausen, 2020; Mandela, 2020; Onyango, 2020; Xinhua, 2019).

Water Supply and Sanitation

The water and sanitation sector in Tanzania is poorly funded relative to the infrastructure, education, health care and agriculture sectors. In fact, the 2016 budget brief indicated that funding for the sector had dropped by 2.4 percent of the overall country budget (United Nations Children's Fund [UNICEF], 2018). The overall state budget has been increasing at a nominal annual average rate of 19.5 percent (and a real annual average growth rate of 10.5 percent). The budget increased from TShs 14.1 trillion in fiscal year 2011/12 to TShs 23 trillion in fiscal year 2015/16 (UNICEF, 2018). The increased expenditure in the sector is reflected in various measures of availability of water supply and sanitation, particularly access to basic drinking water and sanitation in rural and urban areas (see Figure 15).

Despite the increasing trend, there are obvious variations in access based on geographical location and public facilities. Data for the past fifteen years show that on average people in urban areas have better access than those in rural communities. Between 2005 and 2017 about 54 percent and 21 percent of Tanzania's population had access to basic drinking water and sanitation services, respectively (see Table 13). However, when you disaggregate the data by location, about 78 percent of the urban population had access to basic drinking water and 32 percent had access to basic sanitation services. On the other hand, 33 percent and 16 percent of the rural folks had access to basic water and sanitation services, respectively. When you compare Tanzania to the neighboring countries of Ethiopia, Kenya and Uganda, Tanzania is performing on par with its neighbors except Ethiopia, which performs poorly in

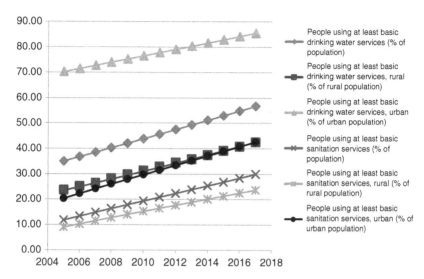

Figure 15 Percentage of people with access to electricity, basic water and
sanitation in Tanzania, 2005–2018
Source: Author's calculations based on World Bank's WDI database

terms of access to basic sanitation. However, all these countries are performing below international standards.

In addition to the differences in access between urban and rural communities, there are stark differences between mainland Tanzania and the Island of
Zanzibar. Ninety-eight percent of the population in Zanzibar have access to
improved drinking water, compared to 86 percent and 49 percent of the urban
and rural mainland, respectively (UNICEF, 2018). Overall, about 61 percent
of Tanzanians have access to improved drinking water, 55 percent use unim-
proved toilet facilities, 16 percent use shared toilet facilities, and only 19 percent have access to improved unshared toilet facilities, while 10 percent do
not use any toilet facility. With regards to schools and health care facilities
where hygiene-related diseases are likely to spread, about 46 percent of
schools lack a functioning water supply, and 84 percent lack handwashing
facilities. In health care facilities only 44 percent of these facilities have
a functioning toilet and only 41 percent have access to improved water
sources (UNICEF, 2018).

During the 2000–2014 period China provided $798,780,012 to finance
forty-two projects in Tanzania's water supply and sanitation sector. These
funds amounted to 3.37 percent of the funding Tanzania received from China
during this period (see Table 12). The projects were funded between 2000
and 2008 and included the construction of: the Chalince rural water supply

Table 13 Percentage of people with access to electricity, basic water and sanitation (averaged over 2005–2018)

	Ethiopia	Kenya	Tanzania	Uganda
Access to electricity (% of population)	35.94	40.19	19.73	18.29
Access to electricity, rural (% of rural population)	24.68	31.37	7.02	10.11
Access to electricity, urban (% of urban population)	86.92	68.23	50.31	50.98
People using at least basic drinking water services (% of population)	34.04	54.98	45.71	40.77
People using at least basic drinking water services, rural (% of rural population)	24.33	45.28	32.74	32.72
People using at least basic drinking water services, urban (% of urban population)	79.18	85.83	77.81	73.43
People using at least basic sanitation services (% of population)	5.93	30.62	20.82	18.23
People using at least basic sanitation services, rural (% of rural population)	3.25	29.15	16.40	15.90
People using at least basic sanitation services, urban (% of urban population)	18.32	35.16	31.51	27.68

Note: Access to electricity is averaged over the 2005–2018 period, while the rest of the indicators are averaged over the 2005–2017 period.
Source: Author's calculations based on World Bank's WDI database

phase one in eleven locations,[15] which was funded in 2000 at a total cost of $361,810,356; phase two of the Chalince water supply was funded in 2007 in the amount of $73,204,170,[16] and the Dodoma city water supply was funded

---

[15] The locations are Pingwe, Msoga, Msata, Miono, Mbwewe, Mbogo, Mazizi, Mandera, Lugoba, Kihangara and Chalince.
[16] Phase two was in Msoga, Msata, Miono, Mbwewe, Mazizi, Mandera, Lugoba, Kidomole and Chalinze.

in 2002 in Dodoma, Makutupora and Chalinze. The Chinese provided additional funding in 2002 for both the Chalince and Dodoma water supplies in the amount of $104,303,824. All financing was classified as grants and the projects were implemented by the China Hainan International Cooperation and the China Guangdong International Corporation. The financing agency was unspecified, recorded as the Chinese government.

In addition to the funds China sent research and training teams to Tanzania in 2008 from the China Urban Construction Design & Research Institute to conduct studies for the Chalince water project. In addition it donated materials to the urban water supply program in Dodoma.

Agriculture, Forestry and Fishing Sector

A total of three projects benefited from Chinese finance in the agriculture, forestry and fishing sector: in 2005 ($245,313 in 2014 US dollars), 2009 ($7,946,222 in 2014 US dollars) and 2012 ($8,191,535 in 2014 US dollars). While the data specify that the projects were funded as grants by a Chinese government institution for the purpose of development, the name of the financing institution is not stated. The 2009 project was construction of agricultural demonstration center and was implemented by the state-owned Chongqing Zhongyi Seed Company. The 2005 grant was recorded as a donation of agricultural machinery (which included three tractors, seven power tillers, two milling machines and two water pumping systems), while the 2012 project involved the development of hybrid rice technology and was recorded as freestanding technical assistance (see Table 14).

In a decision made on June 23, 2006, Wen Jiabao announced China's commitment to build a modern center in Tanzania for agricultural training as a part of a system of ten (increased to twenty in 2009) agrotechnology demonstration centers in Africa. The Sino-Tanzania agrotechnology research and demonstration center was built on a 62 hectare site in Dakawa, Mvomero District in the Morogoro region. The construction and design were completed by the Chongqing Zhongyi Seed Company. The Chinese government reportedly financed the center and provided a Chinese team from the Chongqing Academy of Agricultural Science to manage the center and provide assistance for three years. Construction started on October 28, 2009, and an official handing-over ceremony took place on April 2, 2011. Construction wasn't fully complete until November 2011, however. The finished site has 10 hectares of experimental fields, 2 hectares of offices, laboratory space and training space, and 50 hectares of outside fields equipped with modern irrigation.

Table 14 Chinese funding to agriculture, forestry and fishing sector, 2000–2012

Location	Project Title	Status	Transaction year	flow	Amount (USD defl. 2014)
Tanzania	China Donates Tractors and Water Pumps to Ministry of Agriculture	Completion	2000	Grant	
Tanzania	China Donates Agricultural Machinery to Tanzania	Completion	2005	Grant	$ 245,313.00
Morogoro	China Grants 40 Million CNY to Construct Agricultural Demonstration Center in Tanzania	Completion	2009	Grant	$ 7,946,222.00
Tanzania	China Provides Training Experts in Agriculture for Tanzania	Completion	2006	Free-standing technical assistance	
Morogoro	China Assists Development of Hybrid Rice Technology in Tanzania	Implementation	2012	Free-standing technical assistance	
Dakawa	China Assists Development of Hybrid Rice Technology in Tanzania	Implementation	2012	Free-standing technical assistance	
Tanzania	China Assists Development of Hybrid Rice Technology in Tanzania	Implementation	2012	Free-standing technical assistance	$ 8,191,535.00

Source: Author's calculations based on AidData online database

Government and Civil Society

Between 2003 and 2011 China extended seven grants and five loans to Tanzania in the amount of $259,461,662 (in 2014 US dollars) to finance projects in the government and civil society sector. Two of these seven grants were in-kind grants (for which the exact amount was not specified). The funding agency was again recorded as an unspecified Chinese government institution. In terms of the specific projects, China made various donations that included police vehicles ($440,659), information and computer technology facilities for the Ministry of the Interior ($2,068,370) and computer equipment for the Ministry of Home Affairs ($297,983). The Changzhou City Police Bureau donated laptops to the Tanzania police ($10,035). All of these donations were categorized as grants.

In 2008 China made four loans in the amounts of $46,055,697 each to Tanzania in order to construct the Julius Nyerere Convention Center in Dar es Salaam. In 2013 China extended a grant to Tanzania in the amount of $26,366,130 with which to fund the construction of the Ministry of Foreign Affairs' office building. The Fujian Construction Engineering Group constructed the convention center, while the Anhui Foreign Economic Construction Company group (AFECC) constructed the office building. The Chinese government owns both of these companies.

4 Conclusion and Recommendations

This Element has provided a detailed evaluation of official finances from China to Africa using Tanzania as a case study. Our objective was to provide answers to the following three key questions: How much of Chinese finance is pouring into Africa? Which sectors and projects benefit from these finances? What is Africa's foreign aid policy in relation to Chinese finance? The empirical analysis employed a micro-level approach using data from AidData with a goal of providing in-depth evaluation and targeted policies that could enhance the effectiveness of Chinese finance in the recipient countries.

Distinguishing Features of China's Finance in Africa

I. Indeed, Africa has an infrastructure gap, especially with transportation, energy and ICTs, and a large percentage of Chinese finance funds infrastructure projects. This implies that what China is willing to fund is consistent with Africa's top priority areas. The pattern of financed projects suggests a motivation to facilitate the creation of markets and the export of primary commodities from the continent (Geda, 2018).

II. Relative to funds from OECD member countries, Chinese funds do not come with destabilizing conditions (such as IMF/World Bank structural adjustment programs). However, the majority of the funds are loans, and most of them are funded at market rates, raising the concern of plunging African countries into unstainable debt levels (Geda, 2018; Onjala, 2018).

III. Many of the critiques of China claim that the main motive of Chinese finance in Africa is to access Africa's natural resources. While evidence shows that China is an equal opportunity lender, extending its loans to both resource-rich and resource-poor countries, some of the loans are mortgaged on Africa's natural resources (oil, ores and agricultural output) and future streams of revenues from various projects. The practice of using natural resources as collateral or escrow accounts poses significant risk to many of these countries.

IV. The agricultural sector is the backbone of African countries, yet support for the sector appears negligible. This finding seems to contradict China's own economic model based on "agricultural revolution" for which the current economic transformation and "development miracle" was founded.

V. Chinese firms are implementing the projects, and much of the raw material and labor is imported from China. Aside from the reduced or limited technological transfer and horizontal linkages, there is a potential to create a dependency syndrome where African countries have to continually rely on Chinese experts to maintain these projects (especially infrastructure projects), imposing a big financial constraint on these countries. A very good example is the TaZaRa railway, where both Tanzania and Zambia had to depend on China to maintain the rail since its construction in the 1960s, and the Kiwira Coal Mine in Tanzania.

How Much Chinese Finance Is Pouring into Africa?

Evidence shows that since 2000 China has disbursed more than $86 billion in loans to African countries, with the top five countries being Angola (23 percent), Ethiopia (14 percent), Sudan (6 percent), Kenya (6 percent) and the Democratic Republic of Congo (5 percent) (Hwang, Brautigam and Oem, 2016). These five countries alone accounted for 54 percent of the loans, with the remaining forty-nine countries receiving 46 percent of the loans. The majority of the loans are either funded or managed by two Chinese state banks: Exim Bank (68 percent of the finances) and the CDB (16 percent).

Which Sectors and Projects Benefit from These Finances?

China has funded nearly every sector in Africa with the biggest beneficiaries being infrastructure (56 percent) and mining (10 percent). Projects within the infrastructure sector tend to take the form of constructing new roads or repairing old ones, building or repairing rail lines, renovating or expanding airports, building new harbors or expanding old ones, purchasing airlines and trains, constructing hydroelectric plants, gas power plants and coal power plants, erecting electric transmission lines, gas pipelines and water pipelines and laying inland fiber optics to connect to submarine communication cables. Overall, projects related to transportation, energy and ICTs received 28 percent, 20 percent and 8 percent of the funding, respectively (Hwang et al., 2016).

What Is Africa's Foreign Aid Policy in Relation to Chinese Finance?

Right now Africa does not have an articulated policy on foreign funds, including those from China. Therefore, African countries through the African Union should craft bold and clear policies on China's finance in Africa, covering all facets of their engagements, including foreign aid, investment and trade. These policies should be adopted by regional bodies and modified to meet region-specific needs. Individual countries in the regions could equally adopt a modified policy to fit their country-specific needs. The policies should be in alignment with the continent's long-term development plan. The strength of Africa is its rich natural resources and a growing consumer base, which the rest of the world needs. It should use these strengths strategically as bargaining chips rather than presenting itself like a beggar willing to accept any financing conditions from donor countries with less regard to external debt risks and developmental impact.

The areas that should be clearly spelled out in the policy include:

I. Investment and trade should be mutually beneficial rather than hurt domestic industries. The countries can emphasize specific partnerships with China that can stimulate local industrialization.

II. Preference for Chinese labor versus African labor and general labor market standards. It does not make economic sense for a country to borrow a loan (regardless of the loan conditions) but use labor and material from the funding country to implement the projects funded by that loan. African countries have to bear in mind their high unemployment rates and create avenues for increasing employment.

III. Import of Chinese material for Chinese-funded projects. African countries should require that such imports can only happen if a local alternative is not available.

IV. Taxation and tariffs on Chinese investment and goods should be mutually beneficial.

V. Countries should have a say in the terms of loan repayment that consider the long-term economic risks to individual countries and regions. A clear public debt policy is needed among African countries. African governments should develop clear borrowing policies and bargain for competitive interest rates and accept only favorable bids. Governments should borrow for productive expenditure and manage proceeds from international finances more prudently with integrity and transparency. China should act prudently and support the debt sustainability objectives of African countries.

VI. African countries should provide room for competition with other development partners.

VII. Other issues related to quality of goods and projects, environmental standards and governance issues should be clearly spelled out.

How Can African Countries Maximize Chinese Finances?

In addition to developing a foreign finance policy, African countries should create means to harness the benefits of the expanding infrastructure and other Chinese investments. Underutilized infrastructure will only serve to increase national debt and create inefficiencies in countries where financial resources are scarce. In this regard, African governments could take steps outlined below to enhance the current economic growth momentum and fully take advantage of the expanding infrastructure:

- Formalize the informal sector to create more jobs and increase the tax base – the informal sector accounts for roughly 50–80 percent of GDP and 60–80 of employment and up to 90 percent of new jobs (AfDB, 2018).
- Create an accessible small business fund to encourage new enterprises.
- Reduce/simplify the tax burden on small businesses.
- Build a network of infrastructures that complement each other in order to provide seamless transportation, increase efficiency and reduce transportation costs.
- Find ways to diversify the export sector in order to take advantage of EPZs.

References

African Development Bank (AfDB) (2014). *Africa Economic Outlook 2014: The Global Value Chains and Africa's Industrialization*. Abidjan, Ivory Coast: African Development Bank Group. www.un.org/en/africa/osaa/pdf/pubs/2014afrecooutlook-afdb.pdf

African Development Bank (AfDB) (2015). *Africa Economic Outlook 2015: Regional Development and Spatial Inclusion*. Abidjan, Ivory Coast: African Development Bank Group. www.un.org/en/africa/osaa/pdf/pubs/2014afrecooutlook-afdb.pdf

African Development Bank (AfDB) (2017). *Africa Economic Outlook 2017: Entrepreneurship and Industrialization*. Abidjan, Ivory Coast: African Development Bank Group. www.afdb.org/fileadmin/uploads/afdb/Documents/Publications/AEO_2017_Report_Full_English.pdf

African Development Bank (AfDB) (2018). *Africa Economic Outlook 2018*. Abidjan, Ivory Coast: African Development Bank Group. www.afdb.org/fileadmin/uploads/afdb/Documents/Publications/African_Economic_Outlook_2018_-_EN.pdf

African Development Bank (AfDB) (2019). *Africa Economic Outlook 2019*. Abidjan, Ivory Coast: African Development Bank Group. www.afdb.org/fileadmin/uploads/afdb/Documents/Publications/2019AEO/AEO_2019-EN.pdf

African Development Bank (AfDB) (2020). *Africa Economic Outlook 2020: Developing Africa's Workforce for the Future*. Abidjan, Ivory Coast: African Development Bank Group.

African Development Bank and Organisation for Economic Co-operation and Development (AfDB and OECD) (2006). *Africa Economic Outlook 2005/2006*. Abidjan, Ivory Coast: African Development Bank and Organisation for Economic Co-operation and Development.

African Review (2012). China Signs US$42 Million Tazara Rehabilitation Deal. www.africanreview.com/transport-a-logistics/rail/china-signs-us-42-million-tazara-rehabilitation-deal

Africanews (2017). Djibouti Opens $590 Million World Mega Port Co-funded by China. www.africanews.com/2017/05/25/djibouti-opens-590m-world-class-mega-port-co-funded-by-china

Alden, Chris (2006). China in Africa. *Survival: Global Politics and Strategy* 47(3), 147–164.

Amusa, Kafayat, Nara Monkam and Nicola Viegi (2016). Foreign Aid and Foreign Direct Investment in Sub-Saharan Africa: A Panel Data Analysis. No. 201642. Working Papers, University of Pretoria, Department of Economics.

Atkins, Lucas, Deborah Brautigam, Yunnan Chen and Jyhjong Hwang (2017). Challenges of and Opportunities from the Commodity Price Slump. *SAISI-CARI Economic Bulletin* no. 1. https://static1.squarespace.com/static/ 5652847de4b033f56d2bdc29/t/59f85883ec212d5a70e9624c/150944781259 1/bulletin+v5.pdf

Auty, Richard M. (1994). Industrial Policy Reform in Six Large Newly Industrialising Countries: The Resource Curse Thesis. *World Development* 22(1), 11–26.

Beck, Thorsten and Robert Cull (2014). SME Finance in Africa. *Journal of African Economies* 23(5), 583–613.

Beck, Thorsten, Michael Fuchs and Marilou Uy (2009). Finance in Africa: Achievements and Challenges. World Bank's Policy Research Working Paper WPS5020. http://documents.worldbank.org/curated/en/195001468009290344/ pdf/WPS5020.pdf

Binala, Jaston (2018). Two Love Stories for China from a Dead Coal Mine in Tanzania. *TZ Business News*. www.tzbusinessnews.com/two-love-stories-for -china-from-a-dead-coal-mine-in-tanzania

Bizimungu, Julius (2018). Africa Seeing Rebound in Business Confidence: Report. *New Times*. www.newtimes.co.rw/business/africa-seeing-rebound- business-confidence-report

Bobba, Matteo and Andrew Powell (2007). Aid and Growth: Politics Matters. Inter-American Development Bank. Working Paper No. 601.

Boone, Peter (1996). Politics and the Effectiveness of Foreign Aid. *European Economic Review* 40(2), 289–329.

Brautigam, Deborah (2008). China's Foreign Aid in Africa: What Do We Know? In Robert I. Rotberg (ed.), *China into Africa: Trade, Aid, and Influence*. Washington, DC:Brookings Institution Press, 197–216.

Brautigam, Deborah (2011). Chinese Development Aid in Africa: What, Where, Why, and How Much? In Jane Golley and Ligang Song (eds.), *Rising China: Global Challenges and Opportunities*. Canberra: Australia National University Press, 203–222.

Brautigam, Deborah and Kevin P. Gallagher (2014). Bartering Globalization: China's Commodity-Backed Finance in Africa and Latin America. *Global Policy* 5(3), 346–352.

Brautigam, Deborah and Jyhjong Hwang (2016). Eastern Promises: New Data on Chinese Loans in Africa, 2000–2014. SAIS China-African Research Initiative. Working Paper No. 4.

Burnside, Craig and David Dollar (2000). Aid, Policies, and Growth. *American Economic Review* 90(4), 847–868.

Chen, Maggie X. and Chuanhao Lin (2018). Foreign Investment across the Belt and Road: Patterns, Determinants and Effects. Policy Research Working Paper. WPS8607. World Bank. http://documents.worldbank.org/curated/en/394671539175518256/pdf/WPS8607.pdf

Chen, Yunnan (2019). Ethiopia and Kenya Are Struggling to Manage Debt for Their Chinese-Built Railways. *Quartz Africa*. https://qz.com/africa/1634659/ethiopia-kenya-struggle-with-chinese-debt-over-sgr-railways

Christopoulos, Dimitris K. and Efthymios G. Tsionas (2004). Financial Development and Economic Growth: Evidence from Panel Unit Root and Cointegration Tests. *Journal of Development Economics* 73(1), 55–74.

Collier, Paul and David Dollar (2002). Aid Allocation and Poverty Reduction. *European Economic Review* 46(8), 1475–1500.

Connors, Will (2011). Catering to New Tastes As Incomes Climb. *Wall Street Journal*. www.wsj.com/articles/SB10001424052748704422204576130064161822374

Coulter, Jonathan and Gideon Onumah (2002). The Role of Warehouse Receipt Systems in Enhanced Commodity Marketing and Rural Livelihoods in Africa. *Food Policy* 27(4), 319–337.

Dalgaard, Carl-Johan, Henrik Hansen and Finn Tarp (2004). On the Empirics of Foreign Aid and Growth. *Economic Journal* 114(496), F191–F216.

Dausen, Nuzulack (2019). Tanzania Plans to Extend Its Gas Pipeline Network. Reuters. https://af.reuters.com/article/investingNews/idAFKBN1W11PC-OZABS

Dausen, Nuzulack (2020). Tanzania Signs $1.46 billion Loan for Standard Gauge Railway Construction. Reuters. www.reuters.com/article/us-tanzania-railway/tanzania-signs-1–46-billion-loan-for-standard-gauge-railway-construction-idUSKBN2080JY

Degele, Ergano and Rao Seshagiri (2019). Sino-Africa Bilateral Economic Relation: Nature and Perspectives. *Insight on Africa* 11(1), 1–17.

Deloitte (2016). Africa's Changing Infrastructure Landscape: Africa Construction Trends Report. www2.deloitte.com/content/dam/Deloitte/cn/Documents/international-business-support/deloitte-cn-ibs-africa-construction-report-en-2016.pdf

Deloitte (2019). Capital Projects in a Digital Age: Africa Construction Trends Report. www2.deloitte.com/za/en/pages/energy-and-resources/articles/africa-construction-trends.html

Drake-Brockman, Jane and Sherry Stephenson (2012). Implications for the 21st Century Trade and Development of the Emergence of Services Value Chains. ICTSD. http://ictsd.org/downloads/2012/11/implications-for-21st-century-trade-and-development-of-the-emergence-of-services-value-chains.pdf

Easterly, William (2005). What Did Structural Adjustment Adjust? The Association of Policies and Growth with Repeated IMF and World Bank Adjustment Loans. *Journal of Development Economics* 76(1), 1–22.

Easterly, William, Ross Levine and David Roodman (2004). Aid, Policies, and Growth: Comment. *American Economic Review* 4(3), 774–780.

The Economist (2004). China's Business Links with Africa: A New Scramble. www.economist.com/business/2004/11/25/a-new-scramble

The Economist (2011). The Hopeful Continent – Africa Rising: After Decades of Slow Growth, Africa Has a Real Chance to Follow in the Footsteps of Asia. www.economist.com/leaders/2011/12/03/africa-rising

Edwin, Wilfred (2010). Dar Airport to Handle over 30 Planes an Hour. *The East African*. www.theeastafrican.co.ke/business/2560–870442-y76hjk/index.html

Farole, Thomas and Gokhan Akinci (2011). Special Economic Zones: Progress, Emerging Challenges, and Future Directions. The World Bank. Policy Note No. 63844. http://documents.worldbank.org/curated/en/752011468203980987/pdf/638440PUB0Exto00Box0361527B0PUBLIC0.pdf

Feng, Emily and David Pilling (2019). The Other Side of Chinese Investment in Africa. *Financial Times*. www.ft.com/content/9f5736d8-14e1-11e9-a581-4ff78404524e

Frankel, Jeffrey A. (2010). The Natural Resource Curse: A Survey. NBER Working Paper. WP. No. 15836. www.nber.org/papers/w15836.pdf

French, Howard W. (2014). Why 1 Million Chinese Migrants Are Building a New Empire in Africa. *Quartz*. https://qz.com/217597/how-a-million-chinese-migrants-are-building-a-new-empire-in-africa

Foster, Vivien, William Butterfield, Chen Chuan and Nataliya Pushak (2008). *Building Bridges: China's Growing Role As Infrastructure Financier for Sub-Saharan Africa*. Washington, DC: World Bank.

Gauthier-Villars, David (2011). Mining Fight Shows Pressures on Multinationals. *Wall Street Journal*. www.wsj.com/articles/SB10001424052748703994904575646231168430838

Gebre-Egziabher, Tegegne (2009). The Developmental Impact of Asian Drivers on Ethiopia with Emphasis on Small-Scale Footwear Producers. *World Economy* 32(11), 1613–1637.

Geda, Alemayehu (2018). The Emerging Pattern of African Economic Engagement with China and the Rising South: Implications for Africa's Structural Transformation. *Journal of African Economies* 27(1), i52–i90.

Gettleman, Jeffrey (2016). "Africa Rising"? "Africa Reeling" May Be More Fitting Now. *New York Times*. www.nytimes.com/2016/10/18/world/africa/africa-rising-africa-reeling-may-be-more-fitting-now.html

Glosny, Michael A. (2006). *China's Foreign Aid Policy: Lifting States Out of Poverty or Leaving Them to the Dictators?* Freeman Report. Washington, DC: Center for Strategic and International Studies.

Hamann, Alfonso Javier and Ales Bulir (2001). How Volatile and Unpredictable Are Aid Flows, and What Are the Policy Implications? IMF Working Paper No. 01/167. https://ssrn.com/abstract=292953 or http://dx.doi.org/10.2139/ssrn.292953

Hanauer, Larry and Lyle Morris (2014). *Chinese Engagement in Africa: Drivers, Reactions, and Implications for U.S. Policy.* Santa Monica, CA: Rand Corporation.

Hansen, Henrik and Finn Tarp (2001). Aid and Growth Regressions. *Journal of Development Economics* 64(2), 547–570.

Hollinger Frank, Lamon Rutten and Krassimir Kiriakov (2009). The Use of Warehouse Receipt Finance in Agriculture in ECA Countries. FAO. Technical background paper for the World Grain Forum, St. Petersburg, June 6–7. www.fao.org/3/a-i3339e.pdf

Hubbard, Paul (2008). Chinese Concessional Loans. In Robert I. Rotberg (ed.), *China into Africa: Trade, Aid, and Influence.* Washington, DC: Brookings Institution Press.

Hwang, Jyhjong, Deborah Brautigam and Janet Oem (2016). How Chinese Money Is Transforming Africa: It's Not What You Think. SAISI-CARI Policy Brief No. 11/April 2016. Johns Hopkins School of Advanced International Studies. China Africa Research Initiative.

International Finance Corporation (IFC) (2013). *Warehouse Finance and Warehouse Receipt Systems: A Guide for Financial Institutions in Emerging Economies.* Washington, DC: International Finance Corporation.

International Labour Organization (ILO) (2018). *World Employment and Social Outlook: Trends 2018.* Geneva: International Labour Organization. www.ilo.org/wcmsp5/groups/public/–dgreports/–dcomm/–publ/documents/publication/wcms_615594.pdf

International Monetary Fund (IMF) and World Bank. 2005. *Global Monitoring Report 2005: Millennium Development Goals: From Consensus to Momentum.* Washington, DC: International Monetary Fund and World Bank.

Issahaku, Haruna (2019). Banking Services, Institutions and Economic Growth in Sub-Saharan Africa. In Evelyn F. Wamboye and Peter J. Nyaronga (eds.), *The Services Sector and Economic Development.* London: Routledge, 25–47.

Jiang, Wenran (2008). China's Emerging Strategic Partnerships in Africa. In Robert I. Rotberg (ed.), *China into Africa: Trade, Aid, and Influence.* Washington, DC:Brookings Institution Press, 50–64.

Jordaan, Jacob, Wim Douw and Christine Zhenwei Qiang (2020). What Governments Can Do to Strengthen Linkages and Their Impact. The World Bank Group. http://documents.worldbank.org/curated/en/255331589314877764 /pdf/Foreign-Direct-Investment-Backward-Linkages-and-Productivity-Spillovers-What-Governments-Can-Do-to-Strengthen-Linkages-and-Their-Impact.pdf

Kachiga, Jean (2013). *China in Africa: Articulating China's Africa Policy.* Trenton, NJ: Africa World Press.

Kacungira, Nancy (2017). Will Kenya Get Value for Money from Its New Railway? BBC Africa. www.bbc.com/news/world-africa–40171095

Kagera, Eddy (2017). This Is How SGR Phase 2 Will Look Like: Photos. *Nairobi News.* https://nairobinews.nation.co.ke/news/sgr-phase-2-photos

Karras, Georgios (2006). Foreign Aid and Long-Run Economic Growth: Empirical Evidence for a Panel of Developing Countries. *Journal of International Development* 18(1), 15–28.

Kazungu, Kalume (2018). Youths, Local Industries to Reap More from LAPSSET Project. *Daily Nation.* www.nation.co.ke/news/More-jobs-for-youths-as-Lapsset-project-takes-shape/1056–4867724-a3swecz/index.html

Kiganda, Antony (2017). Djibouti Opens $590m Doraleh Mega Port. *Construction Review Online.* https://constructionreviewonline.com/2017/ 05/djibouti-opens-590m-doraleh-mega-port

Kurlantzick, Joshua (2007). *Charm Offensive: How China's Soft Power Is Transforming the World.* New Haven, CT: Yale University Press.

Lederman, Daniel and William F. Maloney (2003). *Natural Resources and Development: Are They a Curse? Are They Destiny?* Stanford, CA: Stanford University Press.

Lee, Henry and Dan Shalmon (2008). Searching for Oil: China's Oil Strategies in Africa. In Robert I. Rotberg (ed.), *China into Africa: Trade, Aid, and Influence.* Washington, DC: Brookings Institution Press, 109–136.

Leke, Acha, Susan Lund, Charles Roxburgh and Arend van Wamelen (2010). What Is Driving Africa's Growth? Mckinsey and Company. www .mckinsey.com/featured-insights/middle-east-and-africa/whats-driving-afri cas-growth

Lekorwe, Mogopodi, Anyway Chingwete, Mina Okuru and Romaric Samson (2016). China's Growing Presence in Africa Wins Largely Positive Popular Views. Afrobarometer Round 6. Dispatch No. 122/24 October 2016. Afrobarometer.

Levine, Ross Eric (2004). Finance and Growth: Theory and Evidence. NBER Working Paper No. w10766. www.nber.org/papers/w10766

Loxley, John and Harry A. Sackey (2008). Aid Effectiveness in Africa. *African Development Review* 20(2), 163–199.

Lum, Thomas, Hannah Fischer, Julissa Gomez-Granger and Anne Leland (2009). China's Foreign Aid Activities in Africa, Latin America, and South-East Asia. Congressional Research Service Report for Congress. February 25. Washington, DC.

Mahajan, Vijay and Robert E. Gunther (2009). *Africa Rising: How 900 Million African Consumers Offer More Than You Think*. Upper Saddle River, NJ: Prentice Hall.

Mandela, Dominic (2020). Tanzania's Standard Gauge Railway (SGR) to Undergo Formal Testing. *Construction Review Online*. https://constructionre viewonline.com/2020/02/tanzanias-standard-gauge-railway-sgr-to-undergo-formal-testing

Manzano, Osmel and Roberto Rigobon (2001). Resource Curse or Debt Overhang? National Bureau of Economic Research. Working Paper No. 8390. www.nber.org/papers/w8390

Matsiko, Mercy (2012). Tanzania Shuts Operations at Kiwira Coal Mine. *S&P Global*. www.spglobal.com/platts/en/market-insights/latest-news/coal/070412-tanzania-shuts-operations-at-kiwira-coal-mine

Mbogo, Angeline (2018). Uganda Set to Sign Final Financial Deal for Kisumu-Malaba SGR Line. *Kenyan Wall Street*. https://kenyanwallstreet.com/uganda-set-to-sign-final-financial-deal-for-kisumu-malaba-sgr-line

Melick, John and Yan Cheng (2017). The Djibouti Data Center (DDC) Is Selected by China Mobile International Limited (CMI) for Pan African Expansion. Djibouti Data Center. www.djiboutidatacenter.com/en/post/the-djibouti-data-center-ddc-is-selected-by-china-mobile-international-limited-cmi-for-pan-african-expansion

Ministry of Finance and Planning (MoFP) (2016). National Five Year Development Plan 2016/17–2020/21: Nurturing Industrialization for Economic Transformation and Human Development. Ministry of Finance and Planning. United Republic of Tanzania. https://mof.go.tz/mofdocs/mse maji/Five%202016_17_2020_21.pdf

Ministry of Finance and Planning (MoFP) (2018). Speech by the Minister of Finance and Planning, Hon. Dr. Philip I. Mpango (MP), Presenting to the Parliament the Economic Survey Report 2017 and the National Development Plan 2018/19. Ministry of Finance and Planning. United Republic of Tanzania. https://mof.go.tz/docs/Economic%20Survey%20Speech.%202018.19.pdf

Ministry of Finance and Planning (MoFP) (2019). Economic Survey Report, 2018. Ministry of Finance and Planning. United Republic of Tanzania. www.mof.go.tz/docs/THE%20ECONOMIC%20SURVEY%202018.pdf

Ministry of Foreign Affairs of the People's Republic of China (2018). China's Assistance in the Construction of the Tanzania-Zambia Railway. www.fmprc.gov.cn/mfa_eng/ziliao_665539/3602_665543/3604_665547/t18009.shtml

Ministry of Foreign Affairs of the People's Republic of China. www.fmprc.gov.cn/mfa_eng/ziliao_665539/3602_665543/3604_665547/t18001.shtml

Minoiu, Camelia and Sanjay G. Reddy (2009). Development Aid and Economic Growth: A Positive Long Run Relation. IMF. WP/09/118.

Miriri, Duncan (2019). Kenya Opens $1.5 Billion Chinese-Built Railway Linking Rift Valley Town and Nairobi. Reuters. www.reuters.com/article/us-kenya-railway/kenya-opens-chinese-built-railway-linking-rift-valley-town-to-nairobi-idUSKBN1WV0Z0

Moller, Lars Christian and Konstantin M. Wacker (2017). Explaining Ethiopia's Growth Acceleration: The Role of Infrastructure and Macroeconomic Policy. *World Development* 96(C), 198–215.

Moore, Jack (2014). China Railway to Link Kenya, Uganda, Rwanda, Burundi and South Sudan. *International Business Times.* www.ibtimes.co.uk/china-railway-link-kenya-uganda-rwanda-burundi-south-sudan-1448216

Moreira, Sandrina B. (2005). Evaluating the Impact of Foreign Aid on Economic Growth: A Cross-Country Study. *Journal of Economic Development* 30(2), 25–48.

Mourdoukoutas, Panos (2018). What Is China Doing in Africa? *Forbes.* www.forbes.com/sites/panosmourdoukoutas/2018/08/04/china-is-treating-africa-the-same-way-european-colonists-did/#1a8edb11298b

Naim, Moises (2007). Rogue Aid. *Foreign Policy.* March/April (159), 95–96.

Ngugi, Brian (2017). Naivasha-Kisumu SGR Line Takes Shape As State Seeks Nema Nod. *Business Daily Africa.* www.businessdailyafrica.com/economy/Naivasha-Kisumu-SGR-line-takes-shape-as-State-seeks-Nema-nod/3946234-4015918-eucu62z/index.html

Ngwu, Franklin N., Chris I. Ogbechie and Oreva I. Otanya (2019). Insurance Penetration in Sub-Saharan Africa: Issues, Challenges and Prospects. In Evelyn F. Wamboye and Peter J. Nyaronga (eds.), *The Services Sector and Economic Development.* London: Routledge, 11–24.

Niambi, Nathanael T. (2019). China in Africa: Debtbook Diplomacy? *Open Journal of Political Science* 9(1), 220–242.

Obulutsa, George (2019). Tanzania, Zambia Plan $1.5 Billion Oil Products Pipeline: Tanzania Minister. Reuters. www.reuters.com/article/us-tanzania-zambia-pipeline/tanzania-zambia-plan-15-billion-oil-products-pipeline-tan zania-minister-idUSKCN1SY1PT

Onjala, Joseph (2018). China's Development Loans and the Threat of Debt Crisis in Kenya. *Development Policy Review* 36(S2), O710–O728.

Onyango, Emmanuel (2020). Tanzania's SGR on Track after Gov't Secures $1.46 Billion more for Project. *The East African*. www.theeastafrican.co.ke/ business/Tanzania-SGR-on-track-after-govt-secures-loan-for-project/2560– 5456952-i6ki53z/index.html

Organisation for Economic Co-operation and Development (OECD) (2018). Africa's Development Dynamics: Growth, Jobs and Inequalities. African Union Commission and OECD. www.oecd-ilibrary.org/development/africa-s-development-dynamics-2018_9789264302501-en

Organisation for Economic Co-operation and Development (OECD) (2019). Development Aid at a Glance: Statistics by Region. OECD. www.oecd.org/ dac/financing-sustainable-development/development-finance-data/Africa-Development-Aid-at-a-Glance-2019.pdf

Osakwe, Patrick N. (2017). Enhancing the Impact of Chinese Development Finance for Sustained Poverty Alleviation in Africa. In Evelyn Wamboye and Esubalew Tiruneh (eds.), *Foreign Capital Flows and Economic Development in Africa: The Impact of BRICS versus OECD*. New York: Palgrave Macmillan, 69–94.

Oyelaran-Oyeyinka, Banji and Dorothy McCormick (eds.) (2007). *Industrial Clusters and Innovation Systems in Africa*. Tokyo: United Nations University Press.

Park, Yoon J. (2016). One Million Chinese in Africa. John Hopkins School of Advanced International Studies. www.saisperspectives.com/2016issue/ 2016/5/12/n947s9csa0ik6kmkm0bzb0hy584sfo

Porter, Michael E. (1990). The Competitive Advantage of Nations. *Harvard Business Review*. March–April, 73–91.

Pricewaterhouse Coopers (PWC) (2014). Africa Gearing Up: Future Prospects in Africa for the Transportation and Logistics Industry. Pricewaterhouse Coopers. www.pwc.co.za/en/assets/pdf/africa-gearing-up.pdf

Raballa, Victor (2017). SGR Plan Rekindles Hope for Regional Trade in Kisumu. *Daily Nation*. www.nation.co.ke/business/SGR-hope-regional-trade/996–4134342-13wjaxr/index.html

Ramo, Joshua C. (2004). *The Beijing Consensus*. London: Foreign Policy Centre.

Rotberg, Robert I. (2008). China's Quest for Resources, Opportunities and Influence in Africa. In Robert I. Rotberg (ed.), *China into Africa: Trade, Aid, and Influence*. Washington, DC: Brookings Institution Press, 1–20.

Sachs, Jeffrey (2005). *The End of Poverty: Economic Possibilities for Our Time.* New York: Penguin.

Samy, Y. (2010). China's Aid Policies in Africa: Opportunities and Challenges. *Round Table* 99(406), 75–90.

Sedoyeka, Eliamani and John Sicilima (2016). Tanzania National Fibre Broadband Backbone: Challenges and Opportunities. *International Journal of Computing and ICT Research* 10(1), 61–92.

Shepard, Wade (2019). What China Is Really Up to In Africa. *Forbes.* www.forbes.com/sites/wadeshepard/2019/10/03/what-china-is-really-up-to-in-africa/#264f542a5930

Shinn, David H. and Joshua Eisenman (2012). *China and Africa: A Century of Engagement.* Philadelphia: University of Pennsylvania Press.

Signe, Landry (2018). Africa's Consumer Market Potential: Trends, Drivers, Opportunities and Strategies. Africa Growth Initiative at Brookings. www.brookings.edu/wp-content/uploads/2018/12/Africas-consumer-market-potential.pdf

Sisay, Andualem (2019). Kenya, Ethiopia Renew Commitment on LAPSSET. *The East African.* www.theeastafrican.co.ke/business/Kenya-and-Ethiopia-renew-commitment-on-Lapsset/2560–5005358-7cvkjf/index.html

Songwe, Vera (2013). From Bottom Billion to Top Trillion: Using Commodity-Backed Securities to Support the Future of Africa's Resource Economies. Brookings Institute. www.brookings.edu/opinions/from-bottom-billion-to-top-trillion-using-commodity-backed-securities-to-support-the-future-of-africas-resource-economies

Stewart, James (2013). Unintended Consequences: Foreign Aid in Tanzania. United Nations University. https://unu.edu/publications/articles/unintended-consequences-of-foreign-aid-tanzania.html

Sun, Yun (2014). China's Aid to Africa: Monster or Messiah? Brookings Institute. www.brookings.edu/opinions/chinas-aid-to-africa-monster-or-messiah

Svensson, Jakob (1999). Aid Growth and Democracy. *Economics and Politics* 11(3), 275–297.

Taylor, Ian (2006). *China and Africa: Engagement and Compromise.* London: Routledge.

Techerati (2017). China Mobile Selects Djibouti Data Center for African Expansion. Techerati.com. https://techerati.com/the-stack-archive/data-centre/2017/09/05/china-mobile-selects-djibouti-data-center-for-african-expansion

Tiezzi, Shannon (2018). China's Belt and Road Makes Inroads in Africa. *The Diplomat.* https://thediplomat.com/2018/07/chinas-belt-and-road-makes-inroads-in-africa

Tull, Denis M. (2006). China's Engagement in Africa: Scope, Significance and Consequences. *Journal of Modern African Studies* 44(3), 459–479.

United Nations Children's Fund (UNICEF) (2018). Water, Sanitation and Hygiene: Budget Brief, 2018. UNICEF. www.unicef.org/esa/media/2351/file/UNICEF-Tanzania-Mainland-2018-WASH-Budget-Brief-revised.pdf

United Nations Conference on Trade and Development (UNCTAD) (2011). World Investment Report 2011. United Nations Conference on Trade and Development, Geneva. UNCTAD/WIR/2011.

United Nations Conference on Trade and Development (UNCTAD) (2015). World Investment Report 2015. United Nations Conference on Trade and Development, Geneva. UNCTAD/WIR/2015.

United Nations Conference on Trade and Development (UNCTAD) (2017). World Investment Report 2017. United Nations Conference on Trade and Development, Geneva. UNCTAD/WIR/2017.

United Nations Conference on Trade and Development (UNCTAD) (2018). World Investment Report 2018. United Nations Conference on Trade and Development, Geneva. UNCTAD/WIR/2018.

United Nations Conference on Trade and Development (UNCTAD) (2019). World Investment Report 2019. United Nations Conference on Trade and Development, Geneva. UNCTAD/WIR/2019.

United Nations Development Programme (UNDP) (2005). *Human Development Report 2005*. New York: United Nations.

United Nations Development Programme (UNDP) (2017). *African Economic Outlook 2017: Entrepreneurship and Industrialization*. New York: United Nations.

Van Dijk, Meine P. (2017). China's Financial and Aid Flows into Africa and Their Effects. In Evelyn Wamboye and Esubalew Tiruneh (eds.), *Foreign Capital Flows and Economic Development in Africa: The Impact of BRICS versus OECD*. New York: Palgrave Macmillan, 51–68.

Varangis, Panos and Donald Larson (2002). *How Warehouse Receipts Help Commodity Trading and Financing*. Washington, DC:World Bank.

Varangis, Panos, Jean Saint-Geours and Edouard Albert (2017). Using Commodities As Collateral for Finance (Commodity-Backed Finance). World Bank Working Paper No. 117359. https://elibrary.worldbank.org/doi/pdf/10.1596/28318

Wamboye, Evelyn and Rajen Mookerjee (2014). Financial Development and Manufactured Exports: The African Experience. *International Journal of Economic Policy in Emerging Economies* 7(1), 22–34.

Wamboye, Evelyn and Bruno S. Sergi (2019). Exploring the Nature, Motives and Implications of Foreign Capital in Africa. *World Development Perspectives* 14(June), 1–8.

Wang, Fei-Ling and Esi A. Elliot (2014). China in Africa: Presence, Perceptions and Prospects. *Journal of Contemporary China* 23(90), 1012–1032.

Wang, Jian-Ye and Abdoulaye Bio-Tchane (2008). Africa's Burgeoning Ties with China. *Finance and Development* 45(1), 44–47.

World Bank (2014). *Africa Rising: A Tale of Growth, Inequality and Great Promise*. Washington, DC: World Bank. www.worldbank.org/en/news/fea ture/2014/04/14/africa-rising-a-tale-of-growth-inequality-and-great-promise

World Bank (2016). *A Guide to Warehouse Receipt Financing Reform: Legislative Reform*. Washington, DC: World Bank.

World Bank Group (2015). *Tanzania Economic Update: The Elephant in the Room: Unlocking the Potential of the Tourism Industry for Tanzanians*. Dar es Salaam: World Development Bank Africa Region Macroeconomics and Fiscal Management.

World Economic Forum (WEF) (2017). The Africa Competitive Report 2017. World Economic Forum, Geneva. http://documents.worldbank.org/curated/en/733321493793700840/pdf/114750–2-5–2017-15–48-23-ACRfinal.pdf

Xinhua (2015). Chinese-Built Gas Project Launched in Tanzania. State Council: The People's Republic of China. http://english.www.gov.cn/news/top_news/2015/10/12/content_281475209865008.htm

Xinhua (2019). Tanzanian President Inaugurates New Airport Terminal. Xinhuanet. com. www.xinhuanet.com/english/africa/2019–08/02/c_138276384.htm

Cambridge Elements ☰

Economics of Emerging Markets

Bruno S. Sergi
Harvard University

Editor Bruno S. Sergi is an Instructor at Harvard University, an Associate of the Harvard University Davis Center for Russian and Eurasian Studies and Harvard Ukrainian Research Institute. He is the Academic Series Editor of the Cambridge *Elements in the Economics of Emerging Markets* (Cambridge University Press), a co-editor of the *Lab for Entrepreneurship and Development book series, and associate editor of The American Economist*. Concurrently, he teaches International Economics at the University of Messina, Scientific Director of the Lab for Entrepreneurship and Development (LEAD), and a co-founder and Scientific Director of the International Center for Emerging Markets Research at RUDN University in Moscow. He has published over 150 articles in professional journals and twenty-one books as author, co-author, editor, and co-editor.

About the Series

The aim of this Elements series is to deliver state-of-the-art, comprehensive coverage of the knowledge developed to date, including the dynamics and prospects of these economies, focusing on emerging markets' economics, finance, banking, technology advances, trade, demographic challenges, and their economic relations with the rest of the world, as well as the causal factors and limits of economic policy in these markets.

Cambridge Elements ≡

Economics of Emerging Markets

Printed in the United States
by Baker & Taylor Publisher Services